Microsoft®
Word 2016

by Jill Murphy, Custom Performance Solutions

LEVEL 3

LABYRINTH
LEARNING™

Microsoft Word 2016: Level 3

Copyright © 2017 by Labyrinth Learning

Labyrinth Learning
2560 9th Street, Suite 320
Berkeley, California 94710
800.522.9746
On the web at lablearning.com

Product Manager:
Jason Favro

Development Manager:
Laura Popelka

Senior Editor:
Alexandra Mummery

Junior Editor:
Alexandria Henderson

Assessment and Multimedia Content Development:
Ben Linford, Judy Mardar, Andrew Vaughnley

Production Manager:
Debra Grose

Compositor:
Happenstance Type-O-Rama

Indexer:
Valerie Perry

Interior Design:
Debra Grose

Cover Design:
Mick Koller

ebook only ITEM: 1-59136-842-1
ISBN-13: 978-159136-842-7

ebook with printed textbook ITEM: 1-59136-843-X
ISBN-13: 978-159136-843-4

Manufactured in the United States of America

10 9 8 7 6 5 4 3 2

Table of Contents

Preface

This textbook is part of our brand-new approach to learning for introductory computer courses. We've kept the best elements of our proven instructional design and added powerful, interactive elements and assessments that offer enormous potential to engage learners in a new way. We're delighted with the results, and we hope that learners and educators are, too!

Why Did We Write This Content?

In today's digital world, knowing how to use the most common software applications is critical, and those who don't are left behind. Our goal is to simplify the entire learning experience and help every student develop the practical, real-world skills needed to be successful at work and in school. Using a combination of text, videos, interactive elements, and assessments, we begin with fundamental concepts and take learners through a systematic progression of exercises to reach mastery.

What Key Themes Did We Follow?

We had conversations with dozens of educators at community colleges, vocational schools, and other learning environments in preparation for this textbook. We listened and have adapted our learning solution to match the needs of a rapidly changing world, keeping the following common themes in mind:

Keep it about skills. Our content focus is on critical, job-ready topics and tasks, with a relentless focus on practical, real-world skills and common sense as well as step-by-step instruction to ensure that learners stay engaged from the first chapter forward. We've retained our proven method of progressively moving learners through increasingly independent exercises to ensure mastery—an approach that has been successfully developing skills for more than 20 years.

Keep it simple. Our integrated solutions create a seamless and engaging experience built on a uniquely dynamic instructional design that brings clarity to even the most challenging topics. We've focused our content on the things that matter most and have presented it in the easiest way for today's learners to absorb it. Concise chunks of text are combined with visually engaging and interactive elements to increase understanding for all types of learners.

Keep it relevant. Fresh, original, and constantly evolving content helps educators keep pace with today's student and work environments. We have reviewed every topic for relevancy and have updated it where needed to offer realistic examples and projects for learners.

How Do I Use This Book?

We understand that we are in a time of transition and that some students will still appreciate a print textbook to support their learning. Our comprehensive learning solution consists of a groundbreaking interactive ebook for primary content delivery and our easy-to-use eLab course management tool for assessment. We want to help students as they transition to a digital solution. Our interactive ebook contains learning content delivered in ways that will engage learners. Students can utilize a print text supplement in conjunction with the ebook that provides all the textual elements from the ebook in a full-color, spiral-bound print format.

Our eLab platform provides additional learning content such as overviews for each chapter, automatically graded projects and other assessments that accurately assess student skills, and clear feedback and analytics on student actions.

Included with Your Textbook Purchase

▶ *Interactive ebook*: A dynamic, engaging, and truly interactive textbook that includes elements such as videos, self-assessments, slide shows, and other interactive features. Highlighting, taking notes, and searching for content is easy.

▶ *eLab Course Management System*: A robust tool for accurate assessment, tracking of learner activity, and automated grading that includes a comprehensive set of instructor resources. eLab can be fully integrated with your LMS, making course management even easier.

▶ *Instructor resources*: This course is also supported on the Labyrinth website with a comprehensive instructor support package that includes detailed lesson plans, PowerPoint presentations, a course syllabus, test banks, additional exercises, and more.

▶ *Learning Resource Center*: The exercise files that accompany this textbook can be found within eLab and on the Learning Resource Center, which may be accessed from the ebook or online at: **www.labyrinthelab.com/lrc**.

▶ *Overview chapter content*: The "Overview Chapter ISM" folder in the Instructor Support Materials package and the "Overview Chapter Files" folder in the Student Exercise File download include the helpful "Introducing Microsoft Office and Using Common Features" chapter. In addition to providing a discussion of the various Office versions, this chapter introduces a selection of features common throughout the Office applications. **We recommend that students complete this "overview" chapter first.**

We're excited to share this innovative, new approach with you, and we'd love you to share your experience with us at www.lablearning.com/share.

Display Settings

Multiple factors, including screen resolution, monitor size, and window size, can affect the appearance of the Microsoft Ribbon and its buttons. In this textbook, screen captures were taken with at the native (recommended) screen resolutions in Office 2016 running Windows 10, with ClearType enabled.

Visual Conventions

This book uses visual and typographic cues to guide students through the lessons. Some of these cues are described below.

Cue Name	What It Does
`Type this text`	Text you type at the keyboard is printed in this typeface.
Action words	The important action words in exercise steps are presented in boldface.
Ribbon	Glossary terms are highlighted with a light yellow background.
Note! Tip! Warning!	Tips, notes, and warnings are called out with special icons.
⚠	Videos and WebSims that are a required part of this course are indicated by this icon.
Command→Command→ Command→Command	Commands to execute from the Ribbon are presented like this: Ribbon Tab→Command Group→Command→Subcommand.
≡ **Design→Themes→Themes** 🅰	These notes present shortcut steps for executing certain tasks.

Acknowledgements

Many individuals contribute to the development and completion of a textbook. We appreciate the careful attention and informed contributions of Carol Rogers, Accounting Program Chair at Central New Mexico Community College, and Rick Street, Spokane Community College, for their assistance in the development of this book.

We are also deeply grateful to the instructors and professionals who reviewed the text and suggested improvements.

This book has benefited significantly from the feedback and suggestions of the following reviewers:

Pam Silvers, *Asheville-Buncombe Technical Community College*

Ramiro Villareal, *Brookhaven College*

Teresa Loftis, *Inland Career Education Center*

Kim Pigeon, *Northeast Wisconsin Technical College*

Lynne Kemp, *North Country Community College*

Tom Martin, *Shasta College*

Karen LaPlant, *Hennepin Technical College*

Kay Gerken, *College of DuPage*

Colleen Kennedy, *Spokane Community College*

9 | Collaborating in Word

The Internet makes it easy for project teams to collaborate on drafting documents. Team members can exchange documents across the country as easily as across the hall. There are several features that make collaboration activities more efficient. For example, you can track all of the changes made to a document by each team member and combine these changes into a single document for review. In this chapter, you will work with these collaboration tools.

LEARNING OBJECTIVES

- Use the highlighter tool
- Track your changes to a document
- Review tracked changes from others
- Send emails from Word
- Review changes from multiple reviewers
- Compare documents with no tracked changes

🗁 Project: Collaborating on a Manual

As a member of the human resources department, you have been working to finalize the Raritan Clinic East Policies & Procedures Manual. It's now ready for review by personnel in the human resources department. As others review the manual, they will use collaboration tools to mark suggested changes. Some reviewers will insert comments to identify their recommendations, while others will use the Track Changes feature to mark suggested edits. Some will highlight text to identify wording that needs revising. Your task will be to review all suggested edits and comments and finalize the document for printing.

The Highlighter

The highlighter pen works just like its real-life counterpart (except that you can easily erase the highlighting). The pen applies a transparent color to the text background and offers a variety of highlighting colors. You can color-code the highlights you use in a document if you wish. For example, you might highlight a note to yourself in yellow and a "waiting for information" reminder in green.

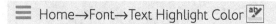 Home→Font→Text Highlight Color

---

DEVELOP YOUR SKILLS: W9-D1

In this exercise, you will highlight a note to yourself and a reminder that you are waiting for additional information from the Finance department.

Before You Begin: *Be sure to visit the Learning Resource Center at labyrinthelab.com/lrc to retrieve the exercise files for this course before beginning this exercise.*

1. Start Word, open **W9-D1-PolicyManual** from your **Word Chapter 9** folder, and save it as `W9-D1-PolicyManualRevised`.

2. Make sure the insertion point is at the beginning of the document and then do a search for *Pediatric General Medicine*.

3. On page 2, position the insertion point in front of *Pediatric*.

4. Type this text and tap ⌷Spacebar⌷ after the period: `Chin has more information about these specialties.`

5. Choose **Home→Font→Text Highlight Color** menu button ▾ and then choose **Bright Green** from the gallery.

   When the mouse pointer is in the body of the document, it looks like a highlighter pen.

6. Drag the pen across the text you just added to highlight it.

7. Choose **Text Highlight Color** to turn off the pen.

   Notice that the color on the button face reflects the most recently used color.

 Tapping ⌷Esc⌷ *also turns off the pen.*

8. Press ⌷Ctrl⌷+⌷End⌷ or scroll down to move to the end of the document and then type this text: `Check with Finance to see if they have information to add.`

9. Select the sentence, choose **Text Highlight Color** 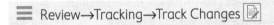 **menu button** ▾, and then choose **Yellow**.

   This highlights the selected text and changes the button color to yellow.

10. Save the file and leave it open.

 Always leave your file open at the end of an exercise unless instructed to close it.

Tracking Changes to a Document

Track Changes is one of the most useful tools for collaborating with team members as you pass documents back and forth. Reviewers can track changes while they edit, and the originator can see who is making what changes in the document and either accept or reject the suggested changes.

Reviewers can also use the Comment feature to leave messages in a document as a means of collaborating with the originator. For example, reviewers may want to explain to the originator why they are making a particular change.

☰ Review→Tracking→Track Changes 📝

📖 Review and Collaboration

You will often have opportunities at school and work to collaborate with others on writing projects. In today's world, when requests for instant feedback are the norm, knowing the typical online reviewing process can ensure that you're well-prepared to be a valuable contributor. Reviewers use Track Changes to mark edits and add comments so reviewers and the originator can converse back and forth. It's important to use Track Changes so the originator can see all of the proposed edits. Files may be passed back and forth among team members via email, cloud storage, or other means. Then the originator can combine the edited documents, accepting and rejecting edits to create the final document.

Viewing Tracked Changes

You have options for viewing edits made to documents using Track Changes. The method you choose is a matter of personal preference.

▸ **Inline:** Edits are marked directly within sentences and paragraphs. Text that is deleted by the reviewer is colored and marked through with a line, and text that is added appears underlined and in a different color.

▸ **Balloons:** Comments and edits appear in balloons on the right side of the document called the markup area. Each balloon identifies the person who made the edit as well as the type of edit made—inserted text, deleted text, and so forth.

 The balloons method is the primary method used in this chapter.

 View the video "Display Options for Track Changes and Comments."

Setting the Username and Initials

Track Changes uses information set up in the Word Options dialog box to identify the username for edits made to a document. As a result, whenever you collaborate on a document in which Track Changes is used, it is important to make sure your username and initials are set correctly.

☰ Review→Tracking→dialog box launcher 🖻 →Change User Name

WORD

Setting Reviewer Ink Colors

Track Changes can use different colors to distinguish the edits of each reviewer who works on the document. Each reviewer can specify colors for his or her comments and tracked changes. This makes it easier to rapidly identify changes submitted by a specific reviewer. It also allows you to keep a consistent color for a reviewer you work with frequently, rather than settling on colors that may be assigned automatically.

≡ Review→Tracking→dialog box launcher 🔲→Advanced Options

DEVELOP YOUR SKILLS: W9-D2

In this exercise, you will turn on Track Changes, change the tracking colors, and set the user's name and initials for the revised Raritan Clinic East policy manual.

1. Choose **Review→Tracking→dialog box launcher** 🔲 and then click the **Advanced Options** button.

2. Follow these steps to choose options for your reviewer ink color settings:

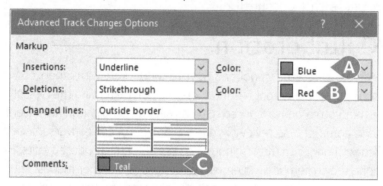

- Ⓐ Set the color for Insertions to **Blue**.
- Ⓑ Set the color for Deletions to **Red**.
- Ⓒ Set the color for Comments to **Teal**.

3. Click **OK**.

4. Click the **Change User Name** button at the bottom of the Track Changes Options dialog box and, if necessary, enter your username and initials.

5. If you want to override the settings from the current Microsoft Account, check the checkbox below the Initials field, Always Use These Values Regardless of Sign In to Office, and then click **OK** twice.

Adding Comments to a Track Changes Document

The Comment feature is a great collaboration tool to use in conjunction with Track Changes. The Reply button in the comment balloon allows reviewers and originators to communicate back and forth during the editing and reviewing process. For example, a reviewer might want to point out the reason for a deletion.

≡ Review→Comments→New Comment 🔲

In this exercise, you will choose the balloon display for tracking changes, and then you will insert a comment and make revisions to the document.

1. Save your file as **W9-D3-PolicyManualRevised**.

2. If necessary, choose **Review→Tracking→Display for Review** and then choose **All Markup** from the menu.

3. Choose **Review→Tracking→Track Changes** and, if necessary, display formatting marks.

4. Choose **Review→Tracking→Show Markup→Balloons** and, if necessary, choose **Show Revisions in Balloons**.

   Deleted text, comments, and formatting changes will appear in balloons in the Markup Area. Added text will be underlined in the body.

5. Scroll to page 2. In the last paragraph on the page, select *Referral* at the beginning of the paragraph.

6. Choose **Review→Comments→New Comment** .

7. Type this text in the comment balloon: **Indent to match other paragraphs.**

8. In the same paragraph, locate and select the text *(see Appendix A)* in the next line and then delete it.

   The deleted text appears in a balloon in the Markup Area, and a gray change bar appears in the left margin to help reviewers locate changes.

9. Follow these guidelines to continue with deletions:
   - Search for the word *see* to locate each additional cross-reference to an appendix.
   - Delete the cross-reference for Appendices B-K.
   - Delete extra spaces between words where appropriate.

10. Search for *Patient Management Procedures* and then position the insertion point at the end of the heading.

11. Follow these steps to insert introductory text for the heading:

    ## Patient·Management·Procedures¶ Ⓐ   Ⓑ

    Ⓒ → It·is·important·that·standard·management·procedures·be·used·to·maintain·the·standards·of· treatment·that·each·patient·deserves.·These·procedures·are·described·in·the·following·pages.¶

    Ⓐ Tap `Enter`.
    Ⓑ Tap `Tab` and then type the text shown here.
    Ⓒ Notice the gray change bar in the left margin that helps locate changes.

    Notice the formatting balloons in the Markup Area. Although the font is the same for the other body text, the style is different from the heading; therefore, the difference is noted.

12. Close the Navigation pane and save the file.

WORD

Reviewing Tracked Changes

Reviewers' tracked changes are only suggestions that don't become permanent unless the originator accepts them. If the originator doesn't agree with a reviewer's suggestion, it can be rejected.

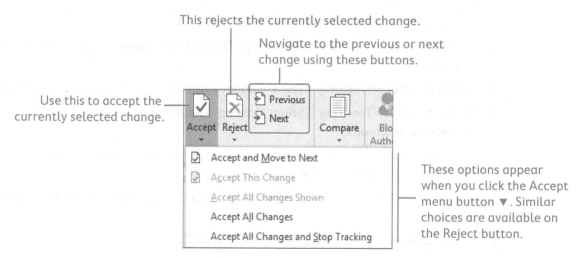

This rejects the currently selected change.

Navigate to the previous or next change using these buttons.

Use this to accept the currently selected change.

These options appear when you click the Accept menu button ▼. Similar choices are available on the Reject button.

 You can right-click a proposed change and choose an Accept or Reject command from the pop-up menu.

Displaying Tracked Changes

You can display tracked changes in four distinctive views. Depending on the type of detail you want to focus on, each view offers specific advantages.

VIEWS FOR TRACKED CHANGES

Markup	Description
Simple Markup	This shows where a change occurred with a red change bar in the margin. Clicking the change bar displays the markup details.
All Markup	This option shows all markups.
No Markup	This hides all markups and displays a final document appearance with the proposed changes.
Original	Select this to show the original document and hide all markups.

≡ Review→Changes→Accept ☑ or Reject ☒

≡ Review→Tracking→Display for Review 📑

DEVELOP YOUR SKILLS: W9-D4

In this exercise, you will display the document using different markup views. Then you will review tracked changes to the document, accepting some changes and rejecting others.

1. Save your file as **W9-D4-PolicyManualRevised**.

2. Choose **Review→Tracking→Display for Review** 📑**→Original** and then scroll through the document.

   The document now appears as it did before changes were made.

3. Choose **Display for Review** 📖→**All Markup** and then scroll through the document.

   Notice the balloons in the Markup Area on the right. Deleted text, comments, and formatting changes appear in balloons, while inserted text is underlined in the body.

4. Choose **Display for Review** 📖→**Simple Markup** and then scroll through the document.

   Red change bars appear in the margin where changes occurred. Clicking the change bar displays all of the changes in detail; clicking it again hides the details. This is a good view for a document with lots of changes.

5. Choose **Display for Review** 📖→**No Markup** and then scroll through the document.

   This view helps you see what the final document will look like.

Accept and Reject Changes

6. Position the insertion point at the top of the document.

7. Choose **Review**→**Changes**→**Next** 🔽.

   This turns on All Markup view and then jumps to and highlights the text you added to the document. This is a good addition, so you will accept it.

8. Choose **Accept** ☑.

   The change marks are removed from the new paragraph, and the focus moves to the next change— the formatting balloon associated with the change you just accepted.

9. Choose **Accept** ☑.

10. Choose **Accept** ☑.

11. Choose **Next** 🔽 to skip the comment and move to the next change, the deleted reference to *Appendix A.*

12. Choose **Reject** ☒.

   The deleted text is restored and you move to the next tracked change.

13. Reject each deleted reference to an appendix.

   The insertion point returns to your comment.

14. Choose **Review**→**Comments**→**Delete** 🗨.

15. Choose **Review**→**Tracking**→**Track Changes** 📝 to turn off the feature.

16. Position the insertion point at the beginning of the paragraph starting with *Referral* (bottom of page 2) and tap ⟦Tab⟧ to indent the first line.

17. Save the file.

Saving and Sending Files

Before reviewers can do their jobs, you must get the document to them. You can use the Internet to share your document in several ways, including the following:

▸ Email

▸ Microsoft OneDrive

▸ Network drive

This chapter uses email as the method for sharing files.

Experience shows that it works best to name each copy of a document sent for review with the reviewer's name. Then, as the documents are returned from review, it's easy to track which reviewer sent each one. It's also a good idea to save all reviewer copies in a single folder to keep them together.

≡ File→Share→Email 🗨

DEVELOP YOUR SKILLS: W9-D5

In this exercise, you will send an email with a copy of the policy manual document attached. For this example, you will send the attachment to your own email address.

1. Choose **Review→Tracking→Track Changes** 📝.

   Turning on the feature helps ensure that the reviewers will use Track Changes.

2. Choose **File→Share→Email** 📧 and then choose **Send as Attachment**.

3. Follow these steps to complete the email form:

   If your user ID was not set up as a user with an Outlook account, you will see a message saying that no profiles have been created. If so, just dismiss the message, turn off Track Changes, and read through the rest of the exercise.

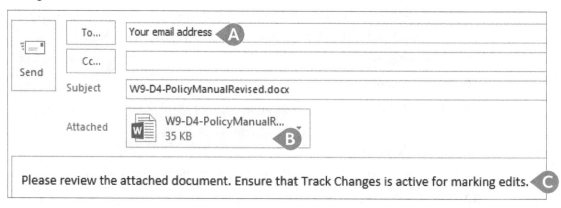

   ⒶEnter your actual email address here (don't type the text shown).

   ⒷVerify that the attachment appears here.

   ⒸAdd this message for the reviewers.

4. Send the email.

5. Choose **Review→Tracking→Track Changes** 📝 to turn off Track Changes.

Reviewing Changes from Multiple Reviewers

If you set up a document to track changes, you can send copies of the document for review by others. As the reviewers make revisions, their changes are tracked. When the reviewers send you their edited copies, you can combine the tracked changes into a single document. Each reviewer's changes are marked in a different color so you can recognize input from different reviewers. After the changes are merged, you can navigate through the combined document and accept or reject edits from all users at one time. In fact, by seeing the edits from all reviewers in one document, you will be able to identify the trouble spots in the document because different reviewers may try to modify the same area of the document.

≡ Review→Compare→Compare 🗐→Combine

Displaying Specific Markups and Reviewers

There are numerous options for displaying tracked changes for combined documents. For example, you may want to look at only the insertions and deletions suggested by reviewers. If you don't need to keep track of formatting changes, you may wish to turn off the Formatting option so you won't be prompted for formatting changes.

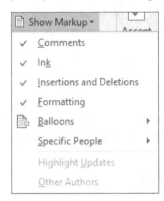

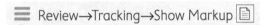
Review→Tracking→Show Markup

If you combine two reviewer documents with the original, you can choose to see changes from both at once, or, at times, you may wish to focus on just one reviewer. You can do that by removing the checkmark in front of the other reviewer's name.

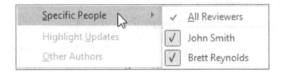

DEVELOP YOUR SKILLS: W9-D6

In this exercise, you will combine proposed changes from two reviewers with the original document. You will also explore additional features used for working with combined documents.

1. Save your file as **W9-D6-PolicyManualRevised**.
2. Choose **Review→Compare→Compare** and then choose **Combine**.
3. Follow these steps to begin combining documents:

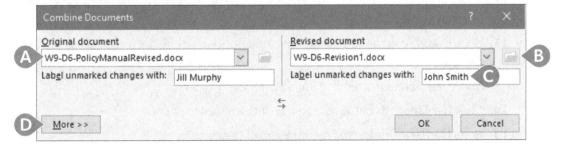

   Ⓐ Choose **W9-D6-PolicyManualRevised** here.

   Ⓑ Click **Browse** and open **W9-D6-Revision1** from your **Word Chapter 9** folder.

   Ⓒ Although there may be another name in this field, type **John Smith** here so you'll know who suggested any unmarked changes.

   Ⓓ Click **More > >** to expand the dialog box.

Note! *If Track Changes is not turned on, the reviewer's name does not appear with the change. Normally changes are tracked, and the name does not need to be entered in the dialog box.*

4. Follow these steps to control document display:

Show changes

Show changes at:	Show changes in:
○ Character level	⦿ Original document **B**
A ⦿ Word level	○ Revised document
	○ New document

(A) Ensure that **Word Level** is active.

(B) Choose **Original Document**.

The Word Level option causes the entire word to be highlighted, even if only one character or punctuation mark changes. This makes it easier to spot small edits. Now John Smith's proposed edits are embedded in the original document, ready for review.

5. Click the **< < Less** button to collapse the dialog box; click **OK**.

Hide Source Documents

6. Click **Compare** 🗐, slide the mouse pointer to **Show Source Documents**, and then, if necessary, choose **Hide Source Documents**.

This provides more room on the screen.

7. Choose **Compare** 🗐 and then choose **Combine**.

8. In the Original Document field, choose **W9-D6-PolicyManualRevised**.

9. Click the **Browse** button next to the Revised Document field and open **W9-D6-Revision2** from your **Word Chapter 9** folder.

10. Type **Brett Reynolds** in the Label Unmarked Changes With field and click **OK**.

Brett Reynolds' edits are now displayed with the original and John Smith's edits.

Turn On the Reviewing Pane

11. If necessary, choose **Review→Tracking→Reviewing Pane** 🖻 **menu button** ▼ and then choose **Reviewing Pane Vertical**.

The Reviewing Pane (labeled Revisions *at the top) summarizes the proposed changes from both reviewers.*

12. Scroll down the Reviewing Pane to the suggested change by Brett Reynolds, where he deleted *attending*.

13. Click *attending* in the Reviewing Pane and notice that the document scrolls to the location of that change.

Notice the Deleted: attending *balloon in the Markup Area.*

14. Click the **Close** ⊠ button at the top of the reviewing pane.

15. Press [Ctrl]+[Home] to move to the top of the document.

16. Review all changes to the document:
    • Delete all comments and accept all formatting changes.
    • Accept all edits by John and Brett with one exception: On page 3, John deleted a space between *(see Appendix B)* and *Children*. Reject that change.

17. Save the file as **W9-D6-Combined** and then close it.

Comparing Documents

Sometimes documents that are sent for review are returned with no visible edits. Reviewers might turn off Track Changes so that the edits they make are not immediately evident. To determine whether edits have been made, you can use the Compare feature. It enables you to merge two documents into one file; then the documents are examined and automatically marked up using Track Changes so you can locate edits.

To Combine or Compare?

The basic procedures are the same for comparing and combining documents, but each command has a different use.

The Combine command allows you to combine the tracked changes from one or multiple reviewers in one document, and then you can go through the single document to accept or reject the changes.

The Compare command is designed for comparing two documents: one edited version of a document, in which the reviewer did not use Track Changes, and the original. If you attempt to use the Compare feature to add a second reviewer's document, you will be advised that it will automatically accept the first person's changes before comparing the second edited document. Thus, you won't have the option of accepting or rejecting changes from the first reviewer.

≡ Review→Compare→Compare ⬚→Compare

DEVELOP YOUR SKILLS: W9-D7

In this exercise, you will compare an original document with a document received from a reviewer that appears to have no changes in it.

1. Open **W9-D6-PolicyManualRevised** from your **Word Chapter 9** folder and save it as **W9-D7-PolicyManualRevised**.

2. Choose **Review→Compare→Compare** ⬚ and then choose **Compare** from the menu.

3. Follow these steps to compare this file with another document:

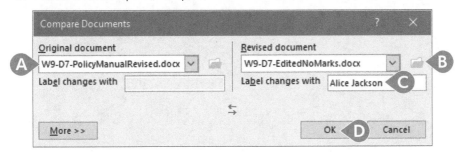

Ⓐ Choose **W9-D7-PolicyManualRevised** as the original document.

Ⓑ Click the **Browse** button for the revised document, navigate to your **Word Chapter 9** folder, and choose **W9-D7-EditedNoMarks**.

Ⓒ Type **Alice Jackson** here to identify the reviewer.

Ⓓ Click **OK** and then click **Yes** if you're asked if you want to continue with the comparison.

4. Scroll through the document and observe Alice's edits.

You won't accept and reject changes in this example.

5. Save the file as **W9-D7-AliceEdits** and exit Word.

Self-Assessment

Check your knowledge of this chapter's key concepts and skills using the Self-Assessment in your ebook or eLab course.

Reinforce Your Skills

REINFORCE YOUR SKILLS: W9-R1

Encourage Good Bugs with Companion Planting

Kids for Change is sponsoring a Master Gardener's seminar, and you have researched companion planting. In this exercise, you will use the highlighter to place reminders in your document, add comments, and track and review changes. You will also email your document as an attachment.

1. Start Word, open **W9-R1-CompanionPlant** from your **Word Chapter 9** folder, and save it as **W9-R1-CompanionPlantRevised**.

2. If necessary, display formatting marks; then position the insertion point at the end of the first paragraph and tap ⎡Enter⎤.

3. Type this text: **Make copies on 3-hole punched paper.**

4. Choose **Home→Font→Text Highlight Color** 🔖 **menu button** ▼**→Turquoise**.

5. Drag the mouse pointer, which now appears as a highlighter pen, across the sentence you just typed.

6. Choose **Text Highlight Color** 🔖 to turn off the highlighter and then position the insertion point at the end of the document.

7. Type this text: **Reminder: Check with Ilsa to see if lupine and savory attract lady bugs.**

8. Select the sentence and then choose **Home→Font→Text Highlight Color menu button** ▼→ **Bright Green**.

Customize Your Track Changes

9. Choose **Review→Tracking→dialog box launcher** 🔲 and then click **Change User Name**.

10. If necessary, enter your username and initials, click **OK**, and then click the **Advanced Options** button.

11. Choose the following colors and then click **OK** twice.
    - Insertions: **Pink**
    - Deletions: **Dark Blue**
    - Comments: **Violet**

Work with Comments and Track Changes

12. Move to the top of the document and select the word *March* in the third line of the first paragraph.

13. Choose **Review→Comments→New Comment** 🗨 and then type this text: **Do we have a specific date yet?**

14. Scroll down to the *Tomatoes + Cabbage* combination and select the last word, *leaves*.

15. Click the **New Comment** button and type this text: **Did Ilsa verify that this combination really works?**

    Now you'll turn on Track Changes and make some editing changes.

16. Choose **Review→Tracking→Track Changes**.

17. In the first sentence below the *Companion Planting* heading on page 1, select *makes for* and type **produces** in its place.

18. In the fifth line of the same paragraph, select *mate* and type **pair** in its place.

19. In the first line of the *Radishes + Spinach* section on page 2, select *yor* and type **your** in its place.

20. Scroll down to the *Collards + Catnip* section, position the insertion point at the end of the sentence, tap Spacebar, and type this text: **And it will make your cat very happy!**

21. Position the insertion point at the end of the *Marigolds and Melons* section and tap Enter.

22. Type this text: **Asparagus + Basil: Seems to encourage lady bugs**.

23. Bold the text *Asparagus + Basil:*.

Now you'll review the tracked changes.

24. Choose **Review→Tracking→Display for Review** 📖 **menu button** ▼**→Original** and scroll through the document.

The document now appears as it was before tracking changes.

25. Use the same technique to experiment with **Simple Markup**, **No Markup**, and **All Markup**, leaving it set at **All Markup**.

Now you will respond to comments and accept and reject the changes as you are playing the role of the reviewer.

26. Position the insertion point at the top of the document.

27. Choose **Review→Changes→Next** 🔲.

The insertion point moves to the first comment.

28. Click **Reply** 💬 in the upper-right corner of the comment balloon and type this text: **I'll check with Ilsa.**

29. Choose **Next** 🔲.

The insertion point moves to the tracked deleted words makes for.

30. Choose **Accept** ☑.

The focus moves to the added word produces.

31. Choose **Accept** ☑.

32. Accept the deletion of *mate* and the addition of *pair*.

The insertion point moves to the added Asparagus + Basil *information.*

33. Choose **Reject** ☒.

The insertion point moves to the next comment.

34. Click **Reply** 💬 in the upper-right corner of the comment balloon and then type this: **I'll check with her.**

35. Choose **Next** 🔲 and accept the deletion of *yor*, the addition of *your*, and accept the "*And it will make your cat very happy!*" addition.

Send a Document for Review

36. Make sure Track Changes is still on.

Remember, you want to ensure that reviewers use Track Changes.

37. Choose **File→Share→Email** 📧 and then choose **Send as Attachment**.

If your user ID was not set up as a user with an Outlook account, you will see a message saying that no profiles have been created. If so, just dismiss the message, turn off Track Changes, and read through the rest of this exercise.

38. In the email form, enter your email address in the To field and then change the **Subject** to **Companion planting document attached for review**.

Notice that the document is already attached.

39. Type this text in the body of the email: **Please be sure Track Changes is turned on when you review the document.**

40. Click **Send** and then choose **Review→Tracking→Track Changes** 📝 to turn it off.

41. Save and close the file.

REINFORCE YOUR SKILLS: W9-R2

Combine and Compare Tracked Changes

Kids for Change is planning to participate in California Coastal Cleanup Day. You've researched some information on why this is important, and now your document has been reviewed by two other members. In this exercise, you will analyze the reviewers' edits and comments to finalize your document.

1. Open **W9-R2-CleanCoast** from your **Word Chapter 9** folder and save it as **W9-R2-CleanCoastRevised**.

2. If necessary, choose **Review→Tracking→Display for Review** 📑 **→All Markup**.

3. Choose **Show Markup** 📄 and then slide the mouse pointer to **Balloons** and, if necessary, choose **Show Only Comments and Formatting in Balloons**.

4. Choose **Review→Compare→Compare** 🗐 **→Combine**.

5. Choose **W9-R2-CleanCoastRevised** from the **Original Document** drop-down list.

6. Click **Browse** on the right side of the dialog box, navigate to your **Word Chapter 9** folder, and open **W9-R2-CleanCoastElla**.

7. Click the **More** button to expand the dialog box and make sure **Word Level** and **Original Document** are chosen, click the **Less** button to collapse the dialog box, and then click **OK**.

8. Choose **Compare** 🗐 and then slide the mouse pointer down to **Show Source Documents** and, if necessary, choose **Hide Source Documents**.

9. Combine the second document, **W9-R2-CleanCoastNed**, with **W9-R2-CleanCoastRevised** and then click **OK**.

10. Position the insertion point at the top of the document and then follow these guidelines to review the changes:

- Accept all additions and deletions made by Ella and Ned.
- Reply to Ned's first comment with: **I'll contact one of the Park School teachers.**
- Reply to Ella's comment with: **We should incorporate that in the report.**
- Reply to Ned's second comment with: **Are you willing to follow up on this?**

11. Save the file as **W9-R2-CoastEllaNed** and then close it.

Compare Docs

12. Open **W9-R2-Pups** from your **Word Chapter 9** folder and save it as **W9-R2-PupsRevised**.

13. Choose **Review→Compare→Compare** 🗐 **→Compare**.

14. Choose **W9-R2-PupsRevised** from the **Original Document** drop-down list.

15. Click the **Browse** button on the right side of the dialog box and open **W9-R2-PupsArthur** from your **Word Chapter 9** folder.

16. Type **Arthur Menendez** in the Label Changes With field on the right and click **OK**.

17. Make sure the insertion point is at the top of the document.

18. Choose **Next** 🖳.

    The first change is a little difficult to see—a comma was added following donors.

19. Accept the change and then continue through the document accepting each addition and deletion.

20. Click **OK** when the message appears indicating there are no more changes.

21. Save the file as **W9-R2-PupsCompare** and then close it.

REINFORCE YOUR SKILLS: W9-R3

Collaborate in Word

Kids for Change will have a booth at a local farmer's market next month where the group will talk about the importance of buying locally grown food. It is preparing a handout that discusses the significance of buying local, and now the document will be reviewed by two members. In this exercise, you will share the file with reviewers using Word's email and then combine tracked changes from two reviewers. Then you will compare another document with a reviewer who forgot to use Track Changes.

1. Open **W9-R3-BuyLocal** from your **Word Chapter 9** folder and save it as **W9-R3-BuyLocalRevised**.

   First, you will turn on Track Changes to ensure that the reviewers use it, and then you will email the document.

2. Choose **Review→Tracking→Track Changes** 📝.

3. Choose **File→Share→Email** 🖼→**Send as Attachment**.

   In this example, you will send the email to yourself. If your user ID was not set up as a user with an Outlook account, you will see a message saying that no profiles have been created. If so, just dismiss the message, turn off Track Changes, and read through the rest of the email portion of the exercise.

4. In the email form, enter your email address in the **To** field and change the **Subject** to **Global research attached**.

   Notice that the document is already attached.

5. Type the following text in the body of the email and then click **Send**:

   Please review and propose any changes you would like.

Combine Tracked Changes from Two Reviewers

6. Choose **Review→Compare→Compare** 🗔→**Combine** and in the Original Document field choose **W9-R3-BuyLocalRevised**.

7. On the right side of the dialog box, click the **Browse** button, open **W9-R3-BuyLocalMarjorie**, and then click **OK**.

8. Choose **Compare** 🗔→**Combine**.

9. In the Original Document field, choose **W9-R3-BuyLocalRevised**.

10. On the right side of the dialog box, browse for and open **W9-R3-BuyLocalSerge** and then click **OK**.

11. If necessary, position the insertion point at the top of the document.

12. Use **Next** and **Accept** to review and accept all proposed changes.

13. Reply to Serge's comment about the number of copies with this text: **I'll check to see how many we made last year.**

14. Reply to Marjorie's comment with this text: **I know she is looking into it. I don't think she has heard back from them yet.**

15. Save the document as **W9-R3-BuyLocalCombined** and then close it.

Compare Documents

Kids for Change will participate in Community Health Week and has prepared a research document on childhood obesity. The document was sent out for review, but the reviewer forgot to use Track Changes, so you will use the Compare feature to locate the changes.

16. Open **W9-R3-Obesity** and save it as **W9-R3-ObesityRevised**.

17. Choose **Review→Compare→Compare** →**Compare**.

18. In the Original Document field, choose **W9-R3-ObesityRevised** and, on the right side of the dialog box, browse for **W9-R3-ObesityMargo**.

19. Type **Margo Meyers** in the Label Changes With field and then click **OK**.

20. Scroll through the document and observe Margo's edits.

    You agree with all of the changes, so you'll accept them all at once.

21. Choose **Accept** menu button ▼→**Accept All Changes**.

22. Save the file as **W9-R3-MargoEdits** and then close it.

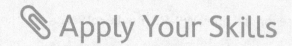 # Apply Your Skills

APPLY YOUR SKILLS: W9-A1

Create a Report on Crete

Universal Corporate Events is adding Crete to its Mediterranean tour offerings. You've prepared a report about Crete, and now you're asking a colleague to review it. In this exercise, you will use the highlighter and Track Changes to edit the document, and then you'll send it on for further review.

1. Open **W9-A1-Crete** from your **Word Chapter 9** folder and save it as **W9-A1-CreteRevised**.

2. Position the insertion point at the end of the paragraph that is below the Crete heading.

3. Tap ⌷Spacebar⌷ and then type this text: **The Roman and Turkish remnants are worth adding to the tour.**

4. Highlight the sentence with pink.

5. Open the **Track Changes Options dialog box**, click **Change User Name**, and, if necessary, enter your username and initials.

6. Click the **Advanced Options** button in the same dialog box and choose these colors:
   • Insertions: **Green**
   • Deletions: **Red**
   • Comments: **Turquoise**

7. Select the city name, *Heraklion*, in the first bullet point.

8. Use the **New Comment** button to insert this comment: **A quick stop in Heraklion to see Knossos would be nice.**

9. Select the city name, *Elounda*, at the beginning of the fifth bullet point and insert this comment: **A good spot for celebrity watching.**

10. Turn on **Track Changes** and, in the fourth line of the paragraph below the *Crete* heading, replace *was* with **were**.

11. In the next line, replace *place* with **island**.

12. In the second line of the second bullet point, replace *Brits* with **British**.

13. Scroll to page 2 and locate the second-from-the-last bullet point about the city of Rethymno.

14. Position the insertion point after the space at the end of the paragraph and type this text: **There is a daily ferry from Athens**.

15. Ensure that **All Markup** is active in the Display for Review field and then position the insertion point at the top of the document.

    Now you'll play the role of the reviewer.

16. Use **Next** and **Accept** to find and accept all editing changes.

17. Create an email using these guidelines:
    - Use Word's Email feature to send the file as an attachment.
    - Insert your email address in the To field.

      If your user ID was not set up as a user with an Outlook account, you will see a message saying that no profiles have been created. If so, just dismiss the message, turn off Track Changes, and read through the rest of this exercise.

    - Change the subject to **Crete Review**.
    - Add this message in the body of the email: **I hope my comments are helpful.**
    - Send the email.

18. Save and close the file.

APPLY YOUR SKILLS: W9-A2

Prepare a Report on Whistler Blackcomb

Universal Corporate Events has a client who wants to reward outstanding employees with a ski vacation, and you've been researching Whistler Blackcomb. In this exercise, you will combine the documents from two reviewers into your original document. Then you will use the Compare feature with a document that was reviewed without Track Changes.

1. Open **W9-A2-Whistler** from your **Word Chapter 9** folder and save it as **W9-A2-WhistlerRevised**.

2. Ensure that the Display for Review feature is set to **All Markup**.

3. Choose **Show Markup→Balloons** and, if necessary, choose **Show Revisions in Balloons**.

4. Combine your original document with Colleen's revised document, **W9-A2-WhistlerColleen**, and enter **Colleen Chase** in the Label Unmarked Changes With field.

5. Combine your original document with Anthony's revised document, **W9-A2-WhistlerAnthony**, and enter **Anthony Nichols** in the Label Unmarked Changes With field.

6. Choose **Compare→Compare**, slide the mouse pointer to **Show Source Documents**, and, if necessary, choose **Hide Source Documents**.

7. Position the insertion point at the top of the document.

8. Accept all changes made by Colleen, Anthony, and Jill, except the change in the first paragraph of the article where Colleen changed kilometers to miles; reject both the deletion and the addition.

9. Save the file as **W9-A2-WhistlerColleenAnthony** and then close it.

   You have researched information about San Diego for a Universal Corporate Events representative, and it has been reviewed by a colleague, Mel. However, Mel did not use Track Changes, so you will use the Compare feature to highlight the changes.

10. Open **W9-A2-SanDiego** from your **Word Chapter 9** folder and save it as **W9-A2-SanDiegoRevised**.

11. Compare **W9-A2-SanDiegoRevised** in the Original Document field with **W9-A2-SanDiegoMel** and type Mel Johnson in the Label Changes With field.

12. Scroll through the document and check the changes.

13. All the changes look good, so accept them all at once.

14. Save the file as **W9-A2-SDCompared** and then close it.

APPLY YOUR SKILLS: W9-A3

Collaborate on a Cabo San Lucas Brochure

Universal Corporate Events has asked you to conduct research for a marketing brochure on Cabo San Lucas. In this exercise, you will make changes to your original document and send it to reviewers. Then you will combine and compare the reviewed documents.

1. Open **W9-A3-Cabo** from your **Word Chapter 9** folder and save it as **W9-A3-CaboRevised**.

2. Make sure **Show Revisions in Balloons** is selected on the Balloons submenu in the Show Markup drop-down list.

3. Open the **Track Changes Options** dialog box and make sure your username and initials appear in the Word Options dialog box.

4. Change the colors in the Advanced Track Changes Options dialog box as follows:
   - Insertions: **Bright Green**
   - Deletions: **Turquoise**
   - Comments: **Dark Red**

5. Turn on **Track Changes**.

6. Below the *See* heading, replace the last word in the first paragraph *abundant* with **plentiful**.

7. In the fourth line of the first bullet point, replace *allows for* with **provides**.

8. In the second line of the next bullet point, enter a comma after *old* and delete the word *and*.

   Now you will review your changes.

9. Position the insertion point at the top of the document and then use the **Next** button to move to and reject the *abundant* deletion and the *plentiful* addition.

10. Accept the rest of the changes.

11. Select *Submarine* in the second bullet point below the heading, *Scuba Diving & Watersports*, and then add this comment: **This looks like a fun activity. Let's check it out.**

12. Save the file.

Check Track Changes Options and Email Files

13. Check that Display for Review is set to **All Markup**.

14. Use the **Email** feature and the **Send as Attachment** option to send the document for review following these guidelines:

    If your user ID was not set up as a user with an Outlook account, you will see a message saying that no profiles have been created. If so, dismiss the message and go to the next step.

    - Enter your own email address in the To field.
    - Change the Subject to **Cabo Review**.
    - Enter this text in the body of the email: **Please make sure Track Changes is turned on**
    - Send the email.

Combine Tracked Changes and Compare Documents

15. Use the combine feature to combine the following documents:
- The original document is **W9-A3-CaboRevised**.
- The first revised document is **W9-A3-CaboAudrey**. (Enter **Audrey Ellis** in the Label Unmarked Changes With field.)
- The second revised document is **W9-A3-CaboJose**. (Enter **Jose Santos** in the Label Unmarked Changes With field.)

16. Accept all changes by Audrey, Jose, and Jill at once.

17. Save the file as **W9-A3-CaboCombo** and then close it.

You recently completed a report on Singapore, which was reviewed by your colleague Ellen. However, she forgot to use Track Changes, so you will use the Compare feature to assess her changes.

18. Open **W9-A3-Singapore** and save it as **W9-A3-SingaporeRevised**.

19. Compare this file with **W9-A3-SingaporeEllen**.

20. Enter **Ellen Pledger** in the **Label Changes With** field.

21. Review the changes and then accept them all.

22. Save the file as **W9-A3-SingCompared** and then close it.

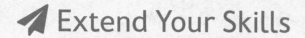 # Extend Your Skills

These exercises challenge you to think critically and apply your new skills. You will be evaluated on your ability to follow directions, completeness, creativity, and the use of proper grammar and mechanics. Save files to your chapter folder. Submit assignments as directed.

W9-E1 That's the Way I See It

Your business professor has assigned you to prepare a report on the best business opportunities for the coming year. To begin, choose a business that appeals to you. Then create a short introduction (4–5 sentences) summarizing your reasons for choosing the business. Search the Internet and copy content of one to two pages on business prospects, citing your sources. Save the file as **W9-E1-Biz**.

Create two copies of the file (**W9-E1-BizJohn** and **W9-E1-BizJorge).** Turn on Track Changes and revise the document using your own ideas. Do the same for the "Jorge" document, making different revisions than you did for John. Combine the revised files with your original file. Note that, because you created the John and Jorge files yourself, your name will appear as the reviewer in all cases. Accept and reject revisions as you see fit and then save and close the file.

W9-E2 Be Your Own Boss

As the owner of Blue Jean Landscaping, you are researching recent articles on business opportunities in landscaping to determine future growth potential. Create a report of one or two pages using online content (citing your sources). Provide a short introductory paragraph (4–5 sentences) summarizing the outlook for the landscaping business. Save your file as **W9-E2-Landscape** and then make a copy, naming it **W9-E2-LandscapeArt**.

Begin to share the document with Art via email from within Word. Fill out the email form. Make up Art's email address and a subject. When complete, tap [PrtScn] and paste the screenshot into a new Word document saved as **W9-E2-Email**. Close the email form without sending. For the "Art" document, revise the document without Track Changes. Insert at least one comment and then save the document. Compare your original with the "Art" file. Note that, because you created the "Art" file yourself, your name will appear as the reviewer. Display the Reviewing Pane in a vertical alignment and then tap [PrtScn]. Add the screenshot to your "Email" document. Accept and reject revisions as you see fit and include a reply to Art's comment. Save and close the file.

W9-E3 Demonstrate Proficiency

Stormy BBQ plans to hold a BBQ Festival. You've been asked to conduct online research to gather ideas for the festival. Using your own ideas and content from online articles, create a report of one or two pages (citing your sources). Provide an introductory paragraph of (4–5 sentences) summarizing the purpose of the festival. Save the report as **W9-E3-Festival** and then make a copy, naming it **W9-E3-FestivalCarla**. Change the reviewer ink setting for insertions, deletions, and comments to red. Tap [PrtScn] and then paste the screenshot of the Advanced Track Changes Options dialog box in a new document saved as **W9-E3-Ink**.

Make revisions to the "Carla" file, including at least one comment and then save it. Combine the "Carla" file with your original. Note that, because you created the "Carla" file yourself, your name will appear as the reviewer. Accept and reject changes as you see fit and insert a reply to the comment. Highlight one sentence with bright green and then save the file.

10 Sharing and Securing Content

In this chapter, you will work in Backstage view to control document access. Online storage, such as OneDrive, allows people to store and retrieve documents from any computer with Internet access, and virtual collaboration means that your documents are often in others' hands. There are features that help you control document content and security and guard your personal information.

LEARNING OBJECTIVES

▸ Use file compatibility features

▸ Check documents with the Document Inspector

▸ Restrict formatting and editing in a document

▸ Mark a document as final

▸ Secure documents with passwords and digital signatures

📁 Project: Securing Confidential Information

At Raritan Clinic East, privacy and security of patient records are vitally important. As a Raritan employee, you will explore features that ensure that documents sent outside the clinic remain confidential and contain no information that could enable those receiving the documents to learn more about patients than they have a need to know. You will use Backstage view and identify some of the security features you can use.

Preparing Documents for Sharing

There are a number of things to think about when sharing documents with colleagues or clients. Compatibility issues between the current and earlier versions of Word should be considered. Additionally, documents can contain hidden or personal information about your organization or about the document that you do not want to share publicly. The Document Inspector can help you deal with these matters.

Compatibility Issues

The most recent versions of Word (2007–2016) use the *.docx* file format. Versions of Word prior to 2007 used a *.doc* file format. Benefits of the latter format include smaller file size, improved damaged-file recovery, and more control of personal information. It's important to understand how the current version of Word behaves with documents created in earlier versions. Likewise, you need to make sure your documents can be read by those using earlier versions. There are several things to think about in dealing with compatibility issues.

▶ The latest versions, Word 2016 and Word 2013, are compatible.

▶ Word 2007, 2010, and 2013 can open *.docx* files created with Word 2016.

▶ Opening a document in Word 2016 that was created in Word 2010 or earlier opens in Compatibility Mode. The features in Word 2016 are downgraded to be compatible with the older versions. The term *[Compatibility Mode]* appears in the title bar.

▶ To open a Word 2016 document in Word 2010 or earlier, you can install the Compatibility Pack for Word, which you can download for free from the Microsoft website.

▶ You can convert documents to Word 2016 that were created in versions prior to Word 2013.

▶ You can save a Word 2016 document as a Word 97-2003 document so it can be opened by users of those versions. Some features of the current version either won't be available or will be modified in a manner more compatible with older versions.

DEVELOP YOUR SKILLS: W10-D1

In this exercise, you will open a Word 2003 document in Word 2016 Compatibility Mode. You will then try to insert a Word 2016 SmartArt graphic (a new feature) in the 2003 document and see how Compatibility Mode deals with this feature.

1. Start Word, open **W10-D1-2003ProcMan** from your **Word Chapter 10** folder, and save it as **W10-D1-2003ProcManRevised**.

   Notice the term [Compatibility Mode] in the title bar at the top of the screen.

   W10-D1-2003ProcManRevised.doc [Compatibility Mode] - Word

   Now you will attempt to add a Word 2016 SmartArt graphic to the Word 2003 Compatibility Mode document.

2. If necessary, display formatting marks and then position the insertion point in front of the paragraph mark at the top of page 2.

3. Choose **Insert→Illustrations→SmartArt** .

   Note that Word opens the Word 2003 Diagram Gallery, rather than the Word 2016 SmartArt gallery, because the Compatibility Mode document cannot work with Word 2016's SmartArt feature.

4. Click **Cancel** to close the Diagram Gallery.

   Next you will observe how Word saves the Compatibility Mode document.

5. Choose **File→Save As** and navigate to your **Word Chapter 10** folder.

   Notice that Word 2016 defaults to the Word 97–2003 format in the Save As Type field. Word 2016 defaults to the older format unless you purposely convert the document to a .docx format or save it as a Word Document (*.docx) via the Save As Type drop-down list.

6. Click **Back** in the upper-left corner to return to the document.

7. Leave the file open.

To Convert or Not to Convert?

If most of the people you share documents with are using pre-2007 versions of Word, it's a good idea to keep their documents in Compatibility Mode. This ensures that documents will look the same in Word 2016 as they do in the older version. It also ensures that the features available in Word 2016 will be limited to, or similar to, the features available in older versions.

Choosing a Conversion Method

If you are working with a Compatibility Mode document that would benefit from the full functionality of Word 2016 features that are currently disabled or limited, you have a candidate for conversion. When you convert the document, Word 2016 turns on the new and enhanced features.

There are two ways to convert an older version (.*doc*) document to a Word 2007-2016 (.*docx*) document:

▸ **Convert:** The Convert command appears on the Info screen in Backstage view when a document is open in Compatibility Mode. Using the command performs a conversion that overwrites the original document. As a result, the older version document is no longer available.

▸ **Save As:** When you resave and rename a document using the Save As command, you are actually making a *copy* of the document. When you perform a Save As with a Compatibility Mode document, you still have the original .*doc* file, and you create a new second file, a .*docx* file.

≡ File→Info→Convert

≡ File→Save As

Consider the User

Always keep the person who sent you the document or the person to whom you are sending a document in mind before converting. If you are editing a document that needs to be returned to someone who is using an earlier version of Word, leave the document in its original format rather than converting it.

The Office Compatibility Pack

People who have earlier versions of Word and who need to work with Word 2016 documents can download a free compatibility pack from the Microsoft website to open, edit, and save Word 2016 documents. However, some features will still not be available.

DEVELOP YOUR SKILLS: W10-D2

In this exercise, you will convert a Word 2003 document to the .docx *format and then add a Word 2016 SmartArt graphic.*

1. Save your file as **W10-D2-2003ProcManRevised**.
2. Choose **File→Info→Convert**.

   A message appears indicting that conversion may cause some minor layout changes. For example, in this document, the pagination is altered slightly when converted.

3. Click **OK** to acknowledge the message.

   Notice that the term [Compatibility Mode] *has disappeared from the title bar.*

4. Position the insertion point on page 2 at the beginning of the first paragraph below the *Scope of Services* heading and make sure the insertion point is to the left of the tab that begins that paragraph.

5. Tap ⌐Enter⌐ and then position the insertion point next to the paragraph mark for the blank line you just created.

6. Choose **Insert→Illustrations→SmartArt** 🖼.

   Because you converted the document, the SmartArt gallery is now available.

7. Follow these steps to insert a SmartArt graphic:

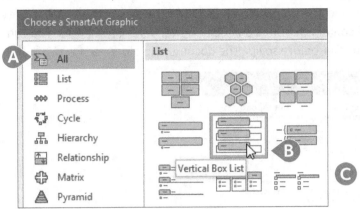

Ⓐ Choose **All** from the category list.

Ⓑ Choose the **Vertical Box List** graphic.

Ⓒ Click **OK**.

8. If necessary, click the tab at the left side of the graphic to open the Type Your Text Here pane.

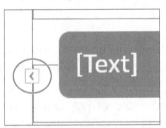

9. Type the text shown:

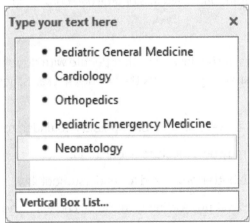

10. Close ☒ the Type Your Text Here pane.

11. Save the document.

Preparing Backward-Compatible Documents

If you know that you'll be working with people who have older versions of Word, and if it's important that all features are compatible among the versions, you might start your new document by saving it as a Word 97–2003 document. That way, you avoid using features unavailable in older versions.

The Compatibility Checker

If you save a Word 2016 document down to an older Word version, the Compatibility Checker notifies you if the document contains features unique to newer versions of Word. You can also manually run the Compatibility Checker before saving the document in older versions.

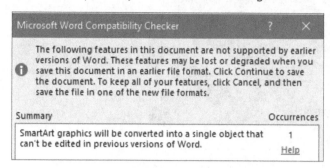

The Compatibility Checker alerts you to how Word 2016 features will be handled if you save a document to an earlier version of Word.

File→Info→Check for Issues→Check Compatibility

Round-Tripping Documents

Round-tripping is a term that you may hear as you work with documents created in various versions of Word. Round-tripping refers to the practice of converting a document to a different format and then saving it back to the original format. For example, you may open a Word *.doc* file, convert it to a *.docx* file, and then decide to save your changes back to a *.doc* format. Round-tripping can create issues with the document that corrupt it so that it acts strangely or is damaged beyond repair.

 Avoid round-tripping your document to prevent unwanted loss of time and data.

The Accessibility Checker

The Accessibility Checker checks elements of the document that people with disabilities may find difficult to read and informs you of the issues so you can fix them. The checker issues errors, warnings, and tips.

▶ **Errors:** Elements of the document may be very difficult or impossible to understand.

▶ **Warnings:** Elements of the document may be difficult to understand.

▶ **Tips:** Elements of the document may be better organized for understandability.

Clicking an item in one of these categories will provide information on changing the content to make it more accessible. There is also a link to Help text that describes in detail what you can do to make documents more accessible.

File→ Info→Check for Issues→Check Accessibility

DEVELOP YOUR SKILLS: W10-D3

In this exercise, you will begin the process to save a Word 2016 document to a Word 97–2003 format version for people who have not yet upgraded. Then you will check for accessibility issues.

1. Choose **File→Save As** and navigate to your **Word Chapter 10** folder.

2. Click the **Save as Type** drop-down list, choose **Word 97–2003 Document**, and click **Save**.

   Word displays the Compatibility Checker with a message indicating that you will not be able to edit the SmartArt graphic, so you've decided not to complete the conversion.

3. Click **Cancel**.

4. Choose **File→Info→Check for Issues→Check Accessibility** to open the Accessibility Checker task pane.

   Notice the two categories: Errors and Tips. There are no warnings for this document.

5. Click the **Read More About Making Documents Accessible** link at the bottom of the task pane to display the Help window.

6. Click the **Creating Accessible Word Documents** link to view the content and then close the Help window and the task pane.

Document Properties and the Document Inspector

Valuable information about a document appears in the Properties panel in Backstage view. Among the data Word stores within a document are the author's name, dates for file creation and editing, and the file storage location. Sending this data along with a document can inadvertently reveal to recipients some data that you would rather protect.

If you intend to share a document with colleagues or clients, you may use the Document Inspector to ensure that it contains no hidden or personal information either in the document itself or in the document properties. For example, a document could contain comments and tracked changes that are hidden from view. Document properties could contain information such as the author's name and the company name.

The Document Inspector will display a list of issues found in a document. The only option for removing data for a category is to remove all data within that category. Sometimes you may want to manually review information before deciding which data to remove.

 Before using the automatic Remove All option for a category, make a copy of the document, run the Document Inspector on the copy, and remove all issues to see the effect. This will help prevent unwanted data loss.

≡ File→Info→Properties

≡ File→Info→Check for Issues→Inspect Document

DEVELOP YOUR SKILLS: W10-D4

In this exercise, you will view document properties and run the Document Inspector. You will remove all personal data from the document.

1. Save your file as **W10-D4-2003ProcManRevised**.

2. Choose **File→Info** and review the properties information in the panel on the right.

   Notice that names appear in the Related People area. You can remove the author's name if desired.

3. Right-click the author's name and choose **Remove Person**.

4. In the Info window, click **Check for Issues** and then choose **Inspect Document**.

5. If prompted to save changes, click **Yes**.

The Document Inspector dialog box opens. You can remove the checkmark from any items you don't want inspected. In this example, you will leave all checkboxes checked.

6. Click **Inspect** at the bottom of the dialog box and review the results.

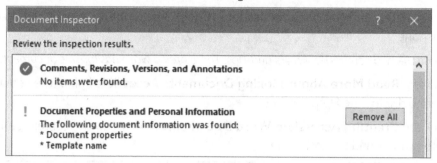

The inspector found document properties.

7. Click **Remove All** to the right of Document Properties and Personal Information and then click **Close**.

8. Choose **File→Info** and notice that, in the Properties panel, all names associated with the document have been removed.

9. Click **Back** ⬅ and save the file.

Controlling Document Access

When you share documents with colleagues and clients, it can be helpful to control the changes that others can make. There are several features to assist you with protecting documents. For example, you can restrict the kinds of formatting and editing changes a reviewer can make. You can add a password to a document, and you can mark a document as final, thereby discouraging changes to it.

Restrict Editing

The Restrict Editing feature enables you to limit editing changes reviewers can make. You also have the option to further limit access with a password.

▸ **Restrict for Tracked Changes:** This setting protects a document from having Track Changes disabled. Every change to the document will be noted. In addition, no one can accept or reject changes while the document is protected.

▸ **Restrict for Comments:** This setting permits reviewers to insert and edit comments in the document but not to edit the document itself.

▸ **Restrict for Filling in Forms:** This setting permits users to insert data only in unrestricted areas of a form.

≡ File→Info→Protect Document→Restrict Editing

DEVELOP YOUR SKILLS: W10-D5

In this exercise, you will set editing restrictions to allow tracked changes, thus preventing reviewers from disabling the feature.

1. Save the file as **W10-D5-2003ProcManRevised**.

2. Choose **File→Info→Protect Document→Restrict Editing** to open the Restrict Editing task pane.

3. Follow these steps to turn on document protection for Tracked Changes:

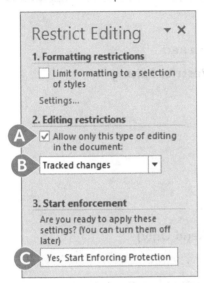

ⓐ Ensure this checkbox is checked.

ⓑ Ensure **Tracked Changes** is chosen here.

ⓒ Click **Yes, Start Enforcing Protection**.

Word displays the Start Enforcing Protection dialog box. At this point, you can either click OK to restrict editing without a password or enter the desired password.

4. Click **OK** to dismiss the password dialog box.

5. On page 2, delete *of Services* in the *Scope of Services* heading.

   The change is marked with Track Changes. No one can alter the document without changes being tracked.

6. Click **Stop Protection** at the bottom of the Restrict Editing task pane.

7. Click **Close** ☒ in the upper-right corner of the Restrict Editing task pane.

8. Choose **Review→Changes→Next** ⬎ and then **Accept** ☑ the change.

9. Click **OK** when the message appears.

10. Save the file.

Allow Changes to Part of a Document

If you choose No Changes (Read Only) in the Editing Restrictions list, the Exceptions option appears where you can specify certain areas of the document that a person can edit freely. For example, if a document is in its final version except for one section, you can exempt the incomplete section of the document so that it can be edited. You can also choose the people you want to allow to edit.

DEVELOP YOUR SKILLS: W10-D6

In this exercise, you will specify the document as read-only; however, you will apply an exception to three paragraphs so reviewers can make changes to them.

1. Save your file as **W10-D6-2003ProcManRevised**.
2. Choose **File→Info→Protect Document→Restrict Editing**.
3. Follow these steps to restrict editing:

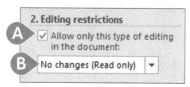

Ⓐ Make sure a checkmark appears here.

Ⓑ Set the restriction level to **No Changes (Read Only)**.

4. Scroll to page 3 and select the three paragraphs below the *Entry into Services* heading.
5. Place a checkmark in the **Everyone** checkbox under Exceptions (Optional).

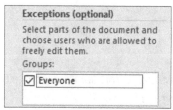

This specifies that all reviewers will be able to edit these paragraphs.

6. Click **Yes, Start Enforcing Protection** at the bottom of the task pane.
7. Click **OK** to bypass setting a password.
8. Click to deselect the paragraphs.

The editable paragraphs are shaded to make them easily visible to reviewers.

Attempt to Edit in a Restricted Area

9. Select a word anywhere there is no shading and tap Delete .

Nothing happens because you are restricted to editing only the shaded paragraphs.

10. Delete the third paragraph in the shaded area.

The deletion is allowed because it is in the area that was specified as an exception.

11. Click **Stop Protection** at the bottom of the task pane.

12. Select the two remaining shaded paragraphs and then remove the checkmark from the **Everyone** checkbox in the task pane.

13. Click in the document and notice the shading has been removed.

14. Save the file.

Restrict Formatting

When you share a document with multiple reviewers, it's easy to imagine a jumble of formats if there are no restrictions. You can restrict reviewers to applying only the Word styles you choose. Formatting is restricted to a list of specified styles, thus providing formatting consistency and preventing anyone from indiscriminately formatting the document.

DEVELOP YOUR SKILLS: W10-D7

In this exercise, you will use the Restrict Editing task pane to apply formatting restrictions.

1. Save your file as **W10-D7-2003ProcManRevised**.

2. Choose **File→Info→Protect Document→Restrict Editing**.

3. Follow these steps to open the Formatting Restrictions dialog box:

ⓐ Place a checkmark here.

ⓑ Click the **Settings** link.

4. Follow these steps to set specific restrictions:

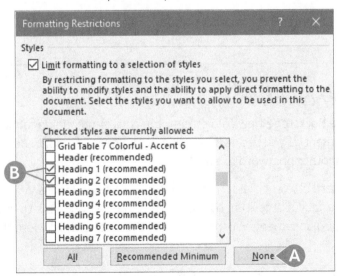

ⓐ Click **None** to uncheck all of the checkboxes at once.

ⓑ Scroll down and place checkmarks in the **Heading 1** and **Heading 2** checkboxes.

The only formatting change a reviewer can make is to add Heading 1 or Heading 2 formatting.

5. Click **OK**, and when Word displays a message asking if you want to remove other styles, click **No**.

   Removing other styles from the document would reformat the entire document, possibly with unexpected results.

6. In section 2 of the Restrict Editing task pane, remove the checkmark next to **Allow Only This Type of Editing in the Document**.

7. Click **Yes, Start Enforcing Protection** in the Restrict Editing task pane.

   In this example, you will not add a password.

8. Click **OK** to dismiss the password dialog box.

   Notice that the task pane now contains a link to Available Styles.

9. Click the **Available Styles** link to display the Styles task pane.

   In addition to the Normal style, the only styles available are Heading 1 and Heading 2.

10. Scroll to the top of page 2 and apply the **Heading 1** style to Our Mission.

11. Close the Styles task pane and then display the **Home** tab.

    Notice that all of the Font and Paragraph formats are grayed out in the Ribbon because formatting is restricted to two heading styles.

12. Click **Stop Protection** at the bottom of the Restrict Editing task pane and then close the task pane.

    Notice that the Font and Paragraph formats are restored on the Ribbon.

13. Save the file.

Passwords and Encryption

By using commands on the Backstage view Info screen, you can set an additional password that is required to open the document. If you use both passwords, the reviewer would need a password to open the document and another password to edit it.

Adding a document password also encrypts the document. Encryption means Word alters information using a code or mathematical algorithm so the information is inaccessible to unauthorized readers. When you encrypt a document, Word prompts you for a password. Note that passwords are case-sensitive.

≡ File→Info→Protect Document→Encrypt with Password

In this exercise, you will set a document password and then remove it.

1. Choose **File→Info→Protect Document→Encrypt with Password**.

2. Type **pass** in the Encrypt Document dialog box and click **OK**.

3. Type **pass** in the Confirm Password dialog box and click **OK**.

   Notice that the security setting is displayed in the Info screen.

4. Click **Back** ⬅ and then save and close the document.

   Depending on the security settings on your computer, you may receive a message asking whether you would like to increase the security. Respond by clicking No.

   Now you'll open the document with a password.

5. Choose **File→Open** and click **W10-D7-2003ProcManRevised** at the top of the Recent Document list.

   In some classrooms, the Recent Documents list may be cleared upon rebooting the computer. If so, navigate to your Word Chapter 10 folder to open the document.

6. Type **pass** in the password box and click **OK**.

   Now you will remove the password.

7. Choose **File→Info→Protect Document→Encrypt with Password**.

8. Select the characters in the password field, tap [Delete], and then click **OK**.

9. Click **Back** ⬅ to return to the document and then save the file.

Marking a Document as Final

Another way to control edits and access to content is to mark the document as "final." Using the Mark as Final command makes a document read-only. As a result, readers and reviewers will know that this document appears as it did when it went to a client, was filed electronically, or was in some other way beyond the point where edits would be useful. Marking as final also prevents accidental altering of the document. When a document is marked as final, the following message appears in the Info tab in Backstage view.

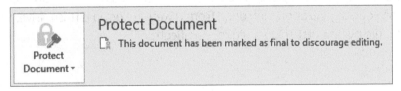

Editing Documents Marked as Final

When the Marked as Final feature is turned on, a yellow bar appears at the top of the document. The message in the bar lets you know that the document has been marked as final to discourage editing, and the Ribbon is hidden. Note that the feature only *discourages* editing. It is not as secure as a password would be. The button in the message bar enables you to edit the document anyway.

ⓘ **MARKED AS FINAL** An author has marked this document as final to discourage editing.		Edit Anyway

☰ File→Info→Protect Document→Mark as Final

DEVELOP YOUR SKILLS: W10-D9

In this exercise, you will mark a document as final and then remove the designation to re-enable editing.

1. Choose **File→Info→Protect Document→Mark as Final**.
2. When Word displays a message that the document will be marked as final and saved, click **OK**.
   Word displays additional information about this setting.
3. Take a moment to read the information and then click **OK**.
   The security setting is displayed on the Info screen.
4. Click **Back** ⊖ to return to the document.
   Notice the Marked as Final *bar at the top of the screen.*
5. Select the heading *Our Mission* on page 2.
6. Tap ⌈Delete⌉ and see that the text is not deleted.
7. Choose **File→Info→Protect Document→Mark as Final** to turn off the feature.
8. Click **Back** ⊖ and notice that the Marked as Final bar at the top of the screen has disappeared.
9. Save the file.

Attaching Digital Signatures

With the capability to rapidly pass documents globally, security concerns may arise. For example, how can a client know for certain that a critical document originated in your office? A digital signature is a secure means of stamping a document as authentic and originating only from you. Other people cannot modify a signed document without removing the digital signature or marking it as invalid.

You may use a digital signature when passing documents to others as an email attachment, as a downloadable file on your organization's intranet, from a website, or on a flash drive. You add a digital signature to a file by first attaching a digital certificate.

Digital Certificates

Digital certificates may be obtained from third-party vendors, who check identification before issuing a certificate. If you post documents on an intranet or the Internet, your network administrator will usually provide you with an authentic digital certificate.

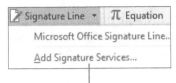

This option on the Signature Line menu links to a Microsoft website, where you can choose a third-party vendor.

You may also create your own digital certificate, although its use is limited. Self-made certificates are not verified by any outside agency; therefore, they're not necessarily a reliable measure, but they are the most convenient.

DEVELOP YOUR SKILLS: W10-D10

In this exercise, you will create a temporary digital certificate on your local computer. You will start by locating the SELFCERT application on your computer, which is installed as part of the Microsoft Office 2016 package.

1. Open **File Explorer** and navigate to the **SELFCERT** application through a path such as C:\Program Files (x86)\Microsoft Office\root\Office16.

Note! *You may need to seek assistance to determine the correct file path for this application on your computer. And note that you may not have user permission to create a digital certificate on computers that are for general use by multiple people.*

2. Scroll to locate the **SELFCERT** application. 🏅 SELFCERT.EXE

3. Double-click the file. When the Create Digital Certification dialog box opens, type **James Elliott** in the **Your Certificate's Name** field.

4. Click **OK**; when a message appears indicating that a certificate was successfully created for James Elliott, click **OK** again.

You have now created a digital certificate that can be used to apply a digital signature to your files.

5. Close the File Explorer window and then save the file.

Digital Signatures

There are two ways to add a digital signature to a document:

▸ You can add a visible signature line to a document and then capture the digital signature when the document is signed.

▸ If a visible signature line is not necessary, you can add an invisible digital signature. A signature button appears on the status bar at the bottom of the screen, so the recipient can verify that the document has a digital signature.

≡ Insert→Text→Signature Line

DEVELOP YOUR SKILLS: W10-D11

In this exercise, you will add a signature line to a document and add a digital signature. You will then attempt to modify the signed document. Finally, you will remove the visible signature and add an invisible digital signature.

1. Save your file as **W10-D11-2003ProcManRevised**.
2. Press ⌈Ctrl⌉+⌈End⌉ to move to the end of the document and then tap ⌈Enter⌉ twice.
3. Choose **Insert→Text→Signature Line** 🖉 to display the Signature Setup dialog box.
4. Complete the information as shown:

The Instructions to the Signer *text is provided by default. You can modify it if necessary. In this exercise, you'll leave the text as it is.*

5. Click **OK** to complete the signature setup.

A signature line appears with the signer's name and title below. Now you'll sign the document.

6. Right-click the signature line and choose **Sign**.

7. Follow these steps to sign the document:

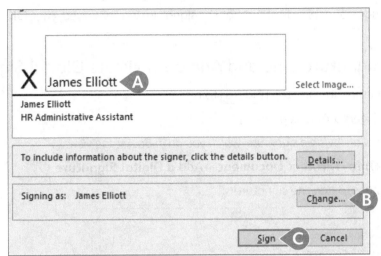

Ⓐ Type **James Elliott** here.

Ⓑ If the Signing As name isn't James Elliott, click **Change**, choose **James Elliott**, and click **OK**. Click **Yes** when the message appears to use the certificate.

Ⓒ Click **Sign**.

If you didn't change the Signing As name, a message appears indicating the certificate cannot be verified and asking whether you want to use this certificate. Remember, a self-created certificate is not verified by a third-party agency.

8. If necessary, click **Yes** to use the certificate.

9. When a message appears indicating your signature has been saved, click **OK**.

A yellow bar appears at the top of the document indicating that the document is marked as final. The Recoverable Signature note above the signature is notifying you that the signature is not verified by an outside agency. A signature button appears on the status bar indicating that there is a digital signature in the document.

10. Attempt to delete a word in the paragraph above the signature line.

A message briefly appears on the status bar indicating that you can't make a change because the selection is locked.

Now you will remove the signature so you can add an invisible signature. Remember, you can use an invisible signature when a visible signature is not required; however, a signature button will still appear on the status bar.

11. Click the signature button on the status bar to display the Signatures task pane.

You may notice the term Recoverable Error *at the top of the task pane. This is because you are using a self-created certificate.*

12. Right-click the **James Elliott** signature in the task pane and choose **Remove Signature**.

A message appears verifying that you want to remove the signature.

WORD

13. Click **Yes** to remove the signature.

14. When a message appears indicating that the signature was removed, click **OK** to dismiss the message.

Remove the Signature Line and Add an Invisible Digital Signature

15. Select the signature line and tap ⌈Delete⌉ to remove it.

16. **Close** ⌈×⌋ the Signatures task pane.

    Now you will add an invisible signature, which you do in Backstage view.

17. Choose **File→Info→Protect Document→Add a Digital Signature**.

18. Follow these steps to add the signature:

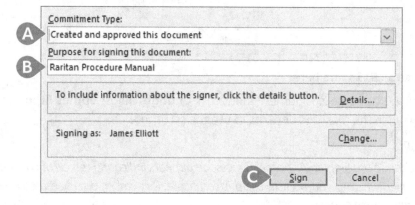

    Ⓐ Choose **Created and Approved This Document**.

    Ⓑ Type **Raritan Procedure Manual** here.

    Ⓒ Click **Sign**.

    A message appears indicating the certificate cannot be verified. Again, a self-created certificate is not verified by a third-party agency.

19. Click **Yes** to use the certificate.

20. When a message appears indicating the signature has been saved with the document, click **OK**.

    Notice the Marked as Final note in the yellow bar at the top of the screen and the signature button on the status bar.

    Because you cannot edit a document after a signature has been attached, there is no option to save the document. When you close the document, the signature will still be attached.

21. Close the file and exit Word.

Self-Assessment

 Check your knowledge of this chapter's key concepts and skills using the Self-Assessment in your ebook or eLab course.

Reinforce Your Skills

REINFORCE YOUR SKILLS: W10-R1

Plan for Trout in the Classroom

Kids for Change hopes to get involved in the "Trout in the Classroom" project, in which kids raise fish from eggs until they are ready to be released in streams. A team member created a research report in Word 2003, but the rest of the team is using Word 2016. In this exercise, you will convert a Word 2003 document to the Word 2016 format, and you will work with backward compatibility, document properties, and the Document Inspector.

1. Start Word, open **W10-R1-Trout** from your **Word Chapter 10** folder, and save it as **W10-R1-TroutRevised**.

   Observe the term [Compatibility Mode] *in the title bar. Now you will attempt to add a SmartArt graphic to the document.*

2. Press ⌈Ctrl⌉+⌈End⌉ to position the insertion point at the end of the document.

3. Choose **Insert→Illustrations→SmartArt** 🖼.

   The Word 2003 Diagram Gallery opens because a Word 2003 document is not compatible with the SmartArt feature.

4. Click **Cancel** to close the Diagram gallery.

   Now you will convert the document to the Word 2016 format.

5. Choose **File→Info→Convert** and click **OK** when the conversion message appears.

   Notice that [Compatibility Mode] *no longer appears in the title bar; the document is now in the Word 2016 format. Now you will insert a SmartArt graphic.*

6. Choose **Insert→Illustrations→SmartArt** 🖼.

7. Choose the **Process** category on the left, choose **Continuous Block Process**, and click **OK**.

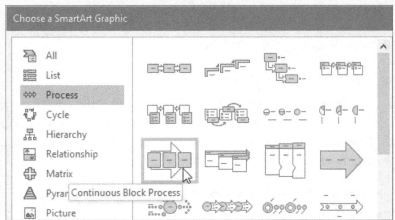

8. Click the tab to the left of the graphic and type the following in the Type Your Text Here pane; close the text pane when you're finished:
   - First bullet: **Hatch**
   - Second bullet: **Release**

9. Click the third text box in the graphic to select it and tap ⌈Delete⌉.

10. Position the mouse pointer on the graphic's upper-right corner sizing handle and then drag down diagonally toward the center of the image until it is about half its original size.

Prepare a Backward-Compatible Document

You want to make sure that the originator of the file will have access to it. You will format a Word 2016 document to be compatible with earlier versions.

11. Choose **File→Save As** and navigate to your **Word Chapter 10** folder.

12. Click the **Save As Type** drop-down list, choose **Word 97-2003 Document (*.doc)**, and click **Save**.

    The Compatibility Checker opens, indicating that SmartArt graphics are not supported in earlier versions of Word. You will cancel the conversion so the SmartArt graphic will work as intended.

13. Click **Cancel**.

Inspect the Document

14. Choose **File→Info** and observe the Properties panel on the right.

    Names appear in the Related People area.

15. In the Info screen, choose **Check for Issues→Inspect Document**.

    A message appears indicating that you should save your changes because the Document Inspector may remove data that can't be restored.

16. Click **Yes** to save the file and open the Document Inspector.

    In this example, you will leave all checkboxes checked.

17. Click **Inspect**.

    The inspector found properties and personal information, which you will remove.

18. Click **Remove All** in the Document Inspector and then close the dialog box.

19. Choose **File→Info** and notice that the names were removed from the Related People area in the Properties panel.

20. Click **Back** ⊙ to return to the document.

21. Save and close the file.

REINFORCE YOUR SKILLS: W10-R2

Help in a Backyard Bee-Counting Project

There has been a decline in the bee population, and Kids for Change plans to help gather data by taking part in a bee-counting project. One of the members has researched methodologies for doing this. The research will be the basis of discussion for the next monthly meeting. In this exercise, you will use document protection features to prevent the document from being modified accidentally.

1. Open **W10-R2-Bees** from your **Word Chapter 10** folder and save it as **W10-R2-BeesRevised**.

2. Chose **File→Info→Protect Document→Restrict Editing** and place a checkmark in the checkbox below the Editing Restrictions heading in the task pane.

3. Choose **Tracked Changes** from the drop-down list and then click **Yes, Start Enforcing Protection**.

4. When the dialog box opens, enter **pass** in both password fields and click **OK**.

5. Select *method* in the first line of the first paragraph below the *Counting the Vanishings Bees* heading and type **technique** in its place.

    The changes are marked because no one can modify the document without changes being tracked.

6. Click **Stop Protection**; when the Unprotect Document box appears, type **pass** in the Password field and click **OK**.

    Now you will accept the changes you made.

7. Choose **Review→Changes→Next** ⬛.

8. **Accept** ☑ both changes and then click **OK** when the message appears.

Apply Editing Restrictions

Now you will apply editing exceptions and specify only certain parts of the document that can be edited. You will, however, allow reviewers to add comments anywhere in the document.

9. Choose **Comments** from the drop-down list in the Editing Restrictions section of the task pane.

10. Select the first three paragraphs in the main article and then place a checkmark in the **Everyone** checkbox below the Exceptions (optional) heading in the task pane.

11. Click **Yes, Start Enforcing Protection** and then click **OK** to close the dialog box without setting a password.

12. Deselect the paragraphs and notice that the unprotected area is shaded, making it easy for reviewers to locate.

13. Select any word outside the shaded section and attempt to delete it.

    The deletion doesn't work because only the shaded area can be edited.

14. In the first line of the third shaded paragraph, select *decline in* and replace it with **waning**.

    The change is allowed because it is in the area specified as an exception. Now you will add a comments as comments were specifically permitted in the Restrict Editing task pane.

15. In the fifth paragraph of the article, select *$200 billion*.

16. Choose **Review→Comments→New Comment** 🗨.

    Comments are allowed, not only in the exceptions area, but anywhere in the document.

17. Type this text: **Can anyone verify this dollar amount?**

18. Click **Stop Protection**.

19. Select the shaded paragraphs; remove the checkmark from the **Everyone** checkbox in the task pane and then close the task pane.

20. Right-click the comment in the markup area and choose **Delete Comment**.

Set a Document Password and Mark a Document as Final

21. Choose **File→Info→Protect Document→Encrypt with Password**.

22. Type **pass** in the Encrypt Document dialog box and click **OK**.

23. Type **pass** in the Confirm Password dialog box, click **OK**, and then save and close the document.

Note! *Depending on the security setting on your computer, you may receive a message asking if you would like to increase the security. Respond by clicking No.*

24. Choose **File→Open** and click **W10-R2-BeesRevised** at the top of the Recent Documents list.

25. Type **pass** in the password box and click **OK**.

26. In the Backstage Info screen, choose **Protect Document** again and choose **Mark as Final**; when the message appears, click **OK**.

27. When additional information about this setting appears, click **OK**.

28. Click **Back** ← to return to the document.

    Notice the Marked as Final bar at the top of the screen.

29. Select the first paragraph in the main article and tap ⌷Delete⌷.

    The text is not deleted because the document is marked as final.

30. Choose **File→Info→Protect Document→Mark as Final** to turn off the feature.

31. Click **Back** ←.

    The Marked as Final bar at the top of the document has disappeared.

Create a Digital Certificate and Add a Digital Signature

Now you will generate a self-created digital certificate so you can apply a digital signature to your document. Remember, a self-created certificate is not verified by an outside agency.

32. Open **File Explorer** and navigate to the **SELFCERT** application through a path such as C:\Program Files (x86)\Microsoft Office\root\Office16.

Note! *You may need to seek assistance to determine the correct file path for this application on your computer. And note that you may not have user permission to create a digital certificate on computers that are for general use by multiple people.*

33. Scroll to locate the **SELFCERT** application. 🔲 SELFCERT.EXE

34. Double-click the file; when the Create Digital Certification dialog box opens, type **Charles Eng** in Your Certificate's Name field and click **OK**.

35. When the message appears indicating the certificate was successfully created, click **OK** and then close the File Explorer window.

36. Position the insertion point at the end of the document and choose **Insert→Text→ Signature Line** 📝.

37. Follow these guidelines to complete the information in the dialog box:
    - Suggested Signer: **Charles Eng**
    - Suggested Signer's Title: **Project Manager**
    - Suggested Signer's E-mail Address: **CharlesEng@Kids.com**.
    - Click **OK** to complete the setup.

38. Right-click the signature line and choose **Sign**; type **Charles Eng** next to the X in the Sign dialog box.

39. If the Signing As name at the bottom of the dialog box is not Charles Eng, follow these steps:
    - Click the **Change** button, choose **Charles Eng**, and click **OK** to close the dialog box.

      A message appears indicating the certificate cannot be verified because a self-created certificate is not verified by an outside agency.
    - Click **Yes** to use the certificate.

40. Click the **Sign** button to close the Sign dialog box; click **Yes** to acknowledge that the certificate cannot be verified.

41. Click **OK** when the next message appears.

42. Attempt to delete a word in the document.

The deletion does not work because you cannot edit a signed document.

43. Save and close the document.

REINFORCE YOUR SKILLS: W10-R3

Learn About 4-H

Kids for Change is thinking about partnering with the 4-H organization on a project. One of the members has researched the organization, and the research document will be the basis for discussion in the next monthly meeting. In this exercise, you will prepare a document for sharing by considering compatibility issues and controlling access to the document. Finally, you will apply a digital signature to the document.

1. Open **W10-R3-4H** from your **Word Chapter 10** folder and save it as **W10-R3-4HRevised**.

   Notice the [Compatibility Mode] term in the title bar. Next you will convert this Word 2003 document to a Word 2016 document.

2. Choose **File→Info→Convert**.

3. When the message appears indicating the conversion may cause changes, click **OK**.

   The term [Compatibility Mode] no longer appears in the title bar. Now you will work with the Document Inspector.

4. Choose **File→Info** and notice that names appear in the Related People area of the Properties panel.

5. In the Info screen, choose **Check for Issues→Inspect Document**.

6. When the message to save changes appears, click **Yes**.

7. When the Document Inspector opens, leave all checkboxes checked and then click **Inspect** and review the results.

   The inspector found properties and personal information in the document.

8. Click **Remove All** and then close the Document Inspector.

9. Choose **File→Info** and notice that the names have been removed in the Related People area of the Properties pane.

Restrict Editing and Apply Editing Exceptions

10. In the Backstage Info screen, choose **Protect Document→Restrict Editing**.

11. If necessary, check the checkbox below the Editing Restrictions heading in the task pane and choose **Tracked Changes** from the drop-down list.

12. Click **Yes, Start Enforcing Protection** and then click **OK** to close the dialog box without setting a password.

13. In the first paragraph below the *About 4-H* heading, position the insertion point in front of *universities*, type **colleges and**, and tap Spacebar.

   The changes are marked with Tracked Changes because that was chosen in the Restrict Editing task pane.

14. Click **Stop Protection** and then right-click the tracked change and choose **Accept Insertion**.

15. Choose **No Changes (Read Only)** from the drop-down list in the Editing Restrictions section of the task pane.

16. Select the three paragraphs below the *Cooperative Extension System* heading on page 1 and then check the **Everyone** checkbox in the task pane.

17. Click **Yes, Start Enforcing Protection** and click **OK** to bypass setting a password.

18. Click in the document to deselect the text and notice that the exceptions text is shaded.

19. If necessary, display formatting marks.

20. Position the insertion point next to the paragraph symbol at the end of the third line in the second paragraph.

21. Tap [Delete] twice to combine the paragraphs and then tap [Spacebar].

22. Click **Stop Protection**, select the shaded paragraphs, and then remove the checkmark from the **Everyone** checkbox.

23. Close the Restrict Editing task pane.

Mark the Document as Final

24. Choose **File→Info→Protect Document→Mark as Final**.

25. When a message appears indicating that the document will be marked as final and saved, click **OK**.

26. When the message appears with additional information about this setting, click **OK**.

27. Click **Back** ⊖ to return to the document and notice the Marked as Final bar at the top of the screen.

28. Close the document.

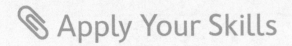

Apply Your Skills

APPLY YOUR SKILLS: W10-A1

Plan a Tour of Mexico City

Universal Corporate Events is planning a tour of Mexico City for a client. The initial research is complete, and now it's time for colleagues to review the article. In this exercise, you will work with compatibility issues, convert a document to different formats, and work with document properties and the Document Inspector.

1. Open **W10-A1-MexCity** from your **Word Chapter 10** folder and save it as
   W10-A1-MexCityRevised.

2. Position the insertion point at the end of the document.

3. Attempt to insert a SmartArt graphic and then use the **Convert** command in Backstage view to convert the document to a **Word 2016 format**.

   Notice that [Compatibility Mode] does not appear in the title bar.

4. Open the **SmartArt Graphic** dialog box, choose the **List** category, and then choose **Vertical Box List** (second graphic in the second row).

5. Open the **Type Your Text Here** pane and add this text at the bullet points:
   - **History**
   - **Economy**
   - **Climate**

6. Close the text pane and then resize the graphic to about half its original size.

7. Use the **Save As** command and navigate to your **Word Chapter 10** folder.

8. Choose **Word 97-2003 Document (*.doc)** from the Save as Type list and then click **Save**.

   When the Compatibility Checker opens, notice that the SmartArt graphic will be converted to an object that can't be edited. You may want to edit the object in the future, so you will prevent the conversion.

9. Click **Cancel**.

   Next, you will work with document properties and the Document Inspector.

10. Go to Backstage view and notice the names in the Related People area in the Properties panel.

11. Use the **Document Inspector** to inspect all categories listed in the dialog box.

12. Remove all document properties and personal information and then close the dialog box.

13. Go to Backstage view and notice that no names appear in the Related People area of the Properties panel.

14. Save and close the file.

Organize a San Francisco Tour

Universal Corporate Events is adding San Francisco to its West Coast tour options. A Universal Corporate Events rep has done some research, and now some other reps who are familiar with San Francisco will review the document. In this exercise, you will use features for securing the document so accidental changes are not made.

1. Open **W10-A2-SanFran** from your **Word Chapter 10** folder and save it as **W10-A2-SanFranRevised**.

2. Open the **Restrict Editing** task pane and restrict editing to **Tracked Changes**.

3. Enforce protection, using **pass** as the password.

   Notice the message in the task pane indicating that all changes will be tracked.

4. Make the following edits:
   - In the fourth line of the first paragraph of the main article, delete *road*.
   - Replace *Within* at the beginning of the second paragraph with **In**.
   - In the second line of the same paragraph, delete the comment in parentheses.

5. Stop protection, enter your password, and accept the changes you made.

   Now you will use formatting restrictions.

6. Apply formatting restrictions that limit formatting to the use of the **Heading 1** style; do not allow other styles to be removed.

7. Start enforcing protection and bypass using a password.

8. Display the available styles and apply the **Heading 1** style to the *Landmarks* and *Neighborhoods* headings.

9. Stop protection and then accept the formatting changes.

   Now you will apply an editing exception.

10. Restrict editing to **Comments** and then select the *Chinatown* paragraph (starts at the bottom of page 1).

11. Check the **Everyone** checkbox to make the paragraph editable by all reviewers.

12. Start enforcing protection and bypass adding a password.

13. Make the following edits:
    - In the first sentence of the *Chinatown* paragraph, delete the phrase *part tourist trap, part*.
    - Select the *Landmarks* heading on page 1 and add this comment:
      A trip to Muir Woods to see giant redwoods is a great side trip.

14. Stop protection, select the *Chinatown* paragraph, and remove the checkmark from the **Everyone** checkbox.

Create a Digital Certificate and Add a Signature

15. Open **File Explorer** and navigate to the **SELFCERT** application.

16. Double-click **SELFCERT** and then type **Ella Mae Chang** in the field at the bottom of the Create Digital Certificate dialog box.

17. Close the **File Explorer** window.

18. Position the insertion point at the end of the document and tap [Enter] twice.

19. Use the **Signature Line** command to open the Signature Setup dialog box.

20. Follow these guidelines to enter the information in the dialog box:
    - Suggested Signer: **Ella Mae Chang**
    - Suggested Signer's Title: **Project Manager**
    - Suggested Signer's E-mail Address: **EllaMae@uce.com**

21. Add **Ella Mae Chang** to the signature line.

    Remember, you may need to change the Signing As name.

22. Attempt to delete a word in the document.

    The deletion is not permitted because a signed document cannot be modified.

23. Delete the signature line in the document.

    Now you will add an invisible signature.

24. Use the **Info** screen in Backstage view to add a digital signature.

25. In the Sign dialog box, choose **Created This Document** from the Commitment Type list.

26. In the **Purpose for Signing This Document** field, type **San Francisco Itinerary**.

27. Click **Yes** to use the certificate; when the message appears indicating the signature has been saved, click **OK**.

28. Close the file.

APPLY YOUR SKILLS: W10-A3

Prepare a Cape Town Itinerary

A Universal Corporate Events rep has conducted some research for a Cape Town travel itinerary. Now some colleagues will review the document. In this exercise, you will prepare the document for sharing. You will consider compatibility issues, apply editing restrictions and exceptions, and add a digital signature.

1. Open **W10-A3-CapeTown** from your **Word Chapter 10** folder and save it as **W10-A3-CapeTownRevised**.

2. Choose **Design→Document Formatting→Themes**.

   This feature is not available in a Word 2003 document. Now you will convert the document to the Word 2016 format.

3. Use the **Convert** command to convert the document to the Word 2016 format.

4. Choose **Design→Document Formatting** and notice that the Themes feature is now available.

   Now you will apply editing and formatting restrictions and formatting exceptions.

5. Apply the **Tracked Changes** editing restrictions, but don't add a password.

6. Make these edits:
   - In the first line of the first paragraph in the main article, replace *neighborhood* with **community**.
   - At the end of the same line, replace *inhabited* with **occupied**.

7. Stop protection and then accept the editing changes.

8. Apply formatting restrictions that limit formatting to the **Heading 1** and **Title** styles; don't allow any other formatting styles in the document to be removed.

9. Enforce protection, but don't set a password.

10. Display the available styles, apply the **Heading 1** style to the *What to See in Cape Town* heading, and then close the Styles task pane.

11. Stop protection and accept the formatting change you made.

    Now you will apply editing exceptions to specify an area of the document where reviewers can freely edit.

12. Restrict editing to **Comments**, select the *Kirstenbosch Botanical Gardens* paragraph at the bottom of page 1, and then check the **Everyone** checkbox.

13. Enforce protection and bypass setting a password.

14. In the fourth line of the editable paragraph, right-click *diverse*, slide the mouse pointer to **Synonyms**, and choose **varied**.

15. Select *Bo-Kaap* at the beginning of the article and add this comment: `I think we should definitely include this in the tour`.

16. Stop protection.

17. Select the exceptions paragraph, remove the checkmark from the **Everyone** checkbox, and then close the task pane.

Add a Digital Signature

18. Open **File Explorer** and navigate to the **SELFCERT** application.

19. Double-click **SELFCERT** and enter `Marty Zane` at the bottom of the Create Digital Certificate dialog box; close the **File Explorer**.

20. Position the insertion point at the end of the document.

21. Set up the signature line with the following information:
    - Suggested Signer: `Marty Zane`
    - Suggested Signer's Title: `Project Manager`
    - Suggested Signer's E-mail Address: `MartyZane@uce.com`

22. Sign the signature line by entering `Marty Zane` next to the X in the Sign dialog box.

23. If necessary, change the Signing As name.

24. Close the document and exit Word.

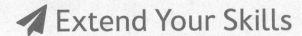

Extend Your Skills

These exercises challenge you to think critically and apply your new skills. You will be evaluated on your ability to follow directions, completeness, creativity, and the use of proper grammar and mechanics. Save files to your chapter folder. Submit assignments as directed.

W10-E1 That's the Way I See It

As the owner of a small business, you are considering adding a new product to your line. Decide on the type of business you are in and what the new product will be. Conduct online research of the new product.

Create a short introduction (3–5 sentences) describing why you think the new product will enhance your line. Copy content of one to two pages about the product, citing your sources. Include at least two headings. Save the file in Word 97-2003 Document (*.*doc*) format as **W10-E1-NewProd**.

Convert the file to the current format. Insert a SmartArt graphic from the List category and list three benefits of your new product. Restrict formatting to Heading 1 and Heading 2 styles and then apply heading styles to all of the headings. Restrict editing to Comments. Select one paragraph and make it exception text that all reviewers may freely edit. Add a comment to text that is not part of the exception text.

W10-E2 Be Your Own Boss

As a member of the marketing team at Blue Jean Landscaping, you are researching online marketing articles specifically targeted to the landscaping business. After researching several articles, decide which marketing approach you will use and write a short introduction (5–6 sentences) describing the benefits of your chosen approach.

Copy the article as the basis for your research document, citing your source. Save the document as **W10-E2-Market**. Because you will be distributing this document to current and potential customers, you want to check it for personal information. Examine the document properties to determine whether your name is visible in the Properties panel. Use the Document Inspector to remove all personal information. Set a document password (**pass**). Finally, create a digital certificate in your name and apply a visible digital signature to the end of the document and sign it.

W10-E3 Demonstrate Proficiency

The owner of Stormy BBQ is considering expanding the business to include a BBQ food truck. Conduct online research regarding how to start a food truck business. Create a one- to two-page report, copying information from the Internet and citing your sources. Write a short introduction (four to five sentences) summarizing why you think a food truck is a good or bad addition to the business. Save the document as **W10-E3-FoodTruck**.

Because you will distribute this document for the Stormy BBQ marketing staff to review, you will prepare it for sharing. Examine your document's properties and use the Document Inspector to remove all personal information. Apply editing restrictions, making it read-only. Enforce protection and assign the password (**pass**). Select a paragraph in the document and apply the exception that makes the paragraph available to all reviewers to edit. Finally, create a digital certificate in your name and apply an invisible digital signature to the document.

WORD

11 | Personalizing Word

As a Word user, you can increase productivity by customizing the application to work the way you want it to work. You can modify Word options and document properties to meet your needs. You can also automate repetitive tasks by recording macros and adapting AutoCorrect to automatically insert text that you use frequently. In this chapter, you will work with Word options, AutoCorrect, document properties, and macros to enhance the way you work.

LEARNING OBJECTIVES

▸ Customize Word options

▸ Use AutoCorrect to insert customized text

▸ Modify document properties

▸ Create and run macros

📁 Project: Setting Up Word to Work the Way You Do

You have been working with Raritan Clinic East for several months. By examining the types of documents you have created during this time, you have some ideas for setting up Word to make it more efficient. You have learned that most documents are saved in folders in a specific location, and you want to set the default directory to access your main folder. You plan to pin documents you use all the time to the Recent Documents list so they are always at the top of the list, and you have discovered that using document properties can be helpful in searching for files located in a large group of files. You have also identified tasks that you perform repeatedly and terms that you type over and over that you will automate.

Setting Word Options

The Word Options dialog box contains numerous options that enable you to control the way Word acts. In the Proofing category, you can set up your own AutoCorrect terms to print. In the Save category, you can change the AutoRecover time interval and identify the default folder you want to use to store files. You can use the Advanced category to set the number of documents that appear in the Recent Documents list.

≣ File→Options

Customizing AutoCorrect

In addition to correcting errors, AutoCorrect lets you automatically insert customized text and special characters. It's also useful for replacing abbreviations with full phrases. For example, you could set up AutoCorrect to insert the name of your company whenever you type an abbreviation for it. And you can delete entries that come with Word that may interfere with your writing; however, this is not recommended when working on public or shared computers, as in improving your own productivity, you may inadvertently complicate that of others.

 View the video "An Overview of the AutoCorrect Dialog Box."

 View the video "AutoCorrect Exceptions."

≣ File→Options→Proofing→AutoCorrect Options button

DEVELOP YOUR SKILLS: W11-D1

In this exercise, you will create a custom AutoCorrect entry. You type Raritan Clinic East *over and over in your work, so it's an ideal candidate for an AutoCorrect shortcut.*

1. Start Word, open **W11-D1-DraftProc** from your **Word Chapter 11** folder, and save it as `W11-D1-DraftProcRevised`.

2. Choose **File→Options**, click the **Proofing** category in the left panel, and then click the **AutoCorrect Options** button to open the AutoCorrect dialog box.

3. Follow these steps to create an AutoCorrect shortcut:

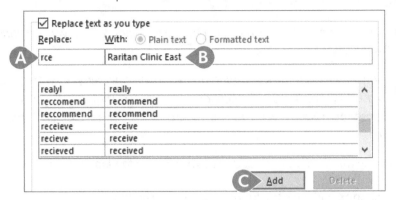

Ⓐ Type **rce** in the Replace field.

Ⓑ Type **Raritan Clinic East** in the With field.

Ⓒ Click **Add**.

4. Click **OK** twice.

5. Press ⎡Ctrl⎤+⎡End⎤ to move to the end of the document and then scroll to the top of the page.

6. In the first line of the first paragraph, position the insertion point in front of the word *share* and type **at** ⎡Spacebar⎤ **rce** ⎡Spacebar⎤.

7. In the first line of the second paragraph, delete *the Clinic*, type **rce** ⎡Spacebar⎤, and correct any spacing if necessary.

Now you will delete the AutoCorrect term so that the next person who uses your computer will have the same experience.

8. Choose **File→Options**, click the **Proofing** category in the left panel, and then click the **AutoCorrect Options** button to open the AutoCorrect dialog box.

9. Type **rce** in the Replace field to scroll the list to that term.

10. Click **Delete** and then click **OK** twice.

11. Save the file.

Changing the AutoRecover Interval and Default File Location

If you are concerned about power failures or are working on an important document, you may wish to reduce the amount of time between automatic saves. Your documents are saved every ten minutes by default.

When Word and other Office programs are installed on a computer, default file locations are set up. The default save location is your OneDrive. If you want to save to a local computer, you can change the save location and reduce the time it takes to navigate to that location. The new save location applies to new, unsaved documents. A document that was previously saved will default to the folder in which it was originally saved.

≡ File→Options→Save→Save AutoRecover Information Every *x* Minutes

≡ File→Options→Save→Default Local File Location

 You may not have user permissions to change the AutoRecover interval or the default file location on a public or shared computer.

In this exercise, you will set the AutoRecover time interval to five minutes. Then you will change the default file location where files are saved.

Before You Begin: *You may need to seek assistance to determine whether you have user permission to change the AutoRecover interval or default file location on computers that are for general use by multiple people. If you do have user permissions, verify the procedure for restoring the original AutoRecover interval and default file location.*

If you are unable to make the changes described, read the steps to familiarize yourself with the process.

1. Choose **File→Options** and click the **Save** category on the left.

 As you make changes, first make a note of the current settings so you can reset them to the original state later in this chapter.

2. Follow these steps to change the AutoRecover interval:

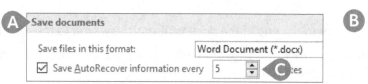

   Ⓐ Locate the **Save Documents** section at the top of the dialog box.

   Ⓑ Write down the current AutoRecover interval so you can reset it later.

   Ⓒ Use the spin box controls to set the time to **5** minutes.

   Your documents will now automatically save every five minutes.

3. In the same section of the dialog box, check the **Save to Computer by Default** checkbox.

4. To specify a particular folder, click the **Browse** button to the right of the Default Local File Location field.

5. In the Modify Location dialog box, scroll in the left column to **Desktop** and then click **OK** twice.

   The Desktop is now your default save location. Next you will test the change.

6. Press ⌈Ctrl⌉+⌈N⌉ to start a new, blank document.

7. Choose **File→Save As** and notice that *This PC* is highlighted rather than OneDrive.

8. Click the **Browse** button at the bottom of the Save As panel on the left.

   The Save As dialog box opens with the Desktop as the target save location.

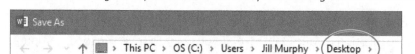

9. Click **Cancel** to close the Save As dialog box and then click **Close** in the left panel to close the blank document.

   If you made changes in this exercise, you will reset them to their original state later in this chapter.

Modifying the Recent Document List

The Open screen in Backstage view displays a list of recent documents accessed on the computer. By default, the Recent Documents list shows the last twenty-five documents opened on the computer. When a document appears in this list, you can open it by clicking the document name. You can turn off the feature so that no documents are listed or change the number of documents shown in the list.

If you move a document to a different folder using an application such as Windows Explorer, the link to the document in the Recent Documents list is broken. After moving a document, you need to re-navigate to the new location to open the file.

Changing the Number of Files in the Recent Documents List

When you work with only a few documents, the documents you need will always appear in the Recent Documents list. If you find that you primarily work with the last few documents before moving on to new documents, you may want to change the number of documents shown to reduce the number of documents you have to select from. Setting the number of documents to display in the list is controlled by settings in the Word Options dialog box. Settings range from zero to fifty.

 View the video "Set the Number of Recent Documents to Display."

≡ File→Options→Advanced→Show This Number of Recent Documents

Pinning a File to the Recent Documents List

Periodically, you may find yourself modifying a document over an extended period of time. To ensure that the document always appears in the Recent Documents list, you can pin it to the list. Pinned documents appear at the top of the list and remain in the list regardless of how many additional documents you access.

 View the video "How to Pin a File to the Recent Documents List."

Clearing the List of Recently Used Documents

Workers who perform tasks associated with specific projects might enjoy the ability to clear all unpinned items from the Recent Documents list, thus displaying only the documents they purposely pinned. In addition, if you are using a computer you share with others, you may want to clear the list so others won't have easy access the documents you used, especially if you work with confidential documents.

 View the video "Setting the Recently Used List to Zero."

 You may not have user permissions to change the Recent documents list on a public or shared computer.

DEVELOP YOUR SKILLS: W11-D3

In this exercise, you will change the number of documents that appear in the Recent Documents list. You will also pin a document to the list.

Before You Begin: *You may need to seek assistance to determine whether you have user permission to change the Recent Documents list. If you do have user permissions, verify the procedure for restoring the original Recent Document settings.*

If you are unable to make the changes described, read the steps to familiarize yourself with the process.

1. Choose **File→Options** and then follow these steps to change the number of documents shown in the Recent Documents list:

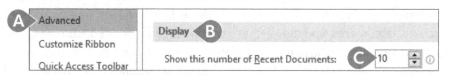

- Ⓐ Choose the **Advanced** category.
- Ⓑ Scroll down to the **Display** options.
- Ⓒ Write down the value in this box and then change the number of documents to **10**.

2. Click **OK** and then choose **File→Open** and note that a maximum of ten documents appear in the Recent Documents list. (Your list may have fewer than ten documents.)

3. Right-click any document in the list and notice (but don't click) the Clear Unpinned Documents command.

   Clicking this would clear all unpinned documents from the list.

4. Tap [Esc] to close the menu.

   Now you will pin, and then unpin, a document in the list.

5. Right-click any document in the list and choose **Pin to List**.

   The document moves to the Pinned category at the top of the list and a pushpin icon appears on the right.

6. Click the pushpin icon of the document you just pinned to unpin it.

7. Click **Back** ⊙ to return to the document window.

Restoring Default Settings

Setting custom options for the way you work is a great practice for a computer that is assigned to you. However, when you are working on a computer you share with others, it is generally a good idea to restore the default settings you have changed.

In this exercise, you will restore the default settings in the Word Options dialog box. By restoring the options to their original state, you also will review the features just covered.

Before You Begin: *Retrieve the default settings you wrote down as you modified options earlier.*

1. Choose **File→Options** and then follow these steps to restore your AutoRecover interval:

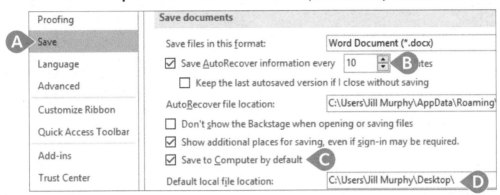

Ⓐ Choose the **Save** category.

Ⓑ Reset the AutoRecover duration to **10**, or enter the setting you wrote down when you made the change in this field.

Ⓒ Uncheck this box if it was previously unchecked.

Ⓓ Enter the file location path you wrote down earlier.

Leave the dialog box open.

2. Follow these steps to restore your Recent Documents list:

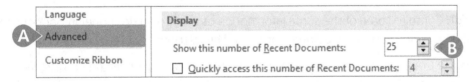

Ⓐ Choose the **Advanced** category.

Ⓑ In the Display section, reset the number of recent documents to **25**, or enter the original setting you wrote down when you made the change in this field.

3. Click **OK**.

Document Properties

Each time you create a new document, properties information is pulled from options set on your computer as well as information detected about the document. Properties information appears in the Properties panel of the Info screen in Backstage view. Information includes such items as the size of the file, the date on which it was created/modified, and the author's name. The Advanced Properties feature contains more data about your document, and this is where you can create custom properties.

The Advanced Properties dialog box contains the widest array of properties.

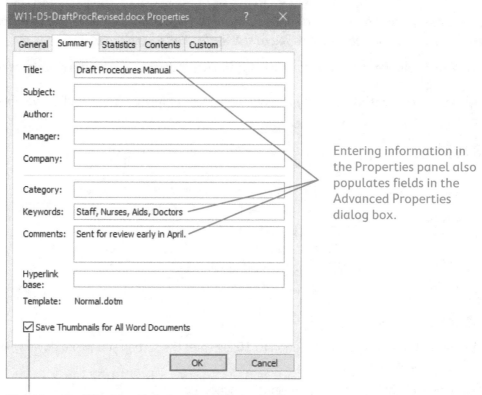

Entering information in the Properties panel also populates fields in the Advanced Properties dialog box.

Checking the "Thumbnails" checkbox fills in the Contents tab with headings (Heading 1 through Heading 3 styles) that appear in the document.

Following are descriptions of the tabs in the Advanced Properties dialog box:

▶ **General:** Contains some of the same information as the Properties panel in Backstage view, as well as additional information, including location and file attributes, such as Read Only

▶ **Summary:** Contains the same text boxes as the Properties panel, including Title, Keywords (Tags), and Comments; checking the Save Thumbnails for All Word Documents checkbox fills in the Contents tab with headings (Heading 1 through Heading 3 styles) that appear in the document

▶ **Statistics:** Contains many of the same statistics as the Properties panel in Backstage view as well as additional fields, such as Paragraphs, Lines, and Characters

▶ **Contents:** Contains the document headings (Heading 1 through Heading 3 styles) when the Save Thumbnails for All Word Documents checkbox is checked on the Summary tab

▶ **Custom:** Allows you to define additional fields, which can be useful when searching for a document in a large group of documents

DEVELOP YOUR SKILLS: W11-D5

In this exercise, you will add comments and keywords (tags) to the procedures manual.

1. Save your file as **W11-D5-DraftProcRevised**.

2. Choose **File→Info** and review the document properties in the Properties panel on the right side of the screen.

3. Enter the information shown in the **Title**, **Tags**, and **Comments** fields and then enter your name in the **Author** field.

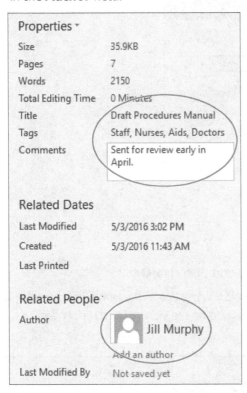

4. Click the **Properties** heading/button at the top of the Properties panel and then click **Advanced Properties**.

   Notice that the properties you entered in the Properties panel are replicated in the Summary tab.

5. Click **OK** and then click **Back** ⬅ to return to the document.

6. Save the file.

Creating a Custom Property

Though the available properties are sufficient for most documents, there may be times when you want to store additional properties. When there is no existing property to meet your needs, you can create a custom property and define the type of data you plan to place in the field, including Text, Date, and Number. A list of suggested names is provided for custom fields, but you can also define your own property names. For example, if you want to include a due date for a document, you can create a new Due Date property and assign Date as the data type. These custom properties don't appear in the Properties panel in the Backstage Info view. To view them, you need to refer to the Custom tab of the Advanced Properties dialog box.

DEVELOP YOUR SKILLS: W11-D6

In this exercise, you will create a custom property for the procedures manual to hold the due date for the final version of the document.

1. Save your file as **W11-D6-DraftProcRevised**.

2. Choose **File→Info**, click **Properties** at the top of the Properties panel, and choose **Advanced Properties**.

3. Follow these steps to create a new custom property:

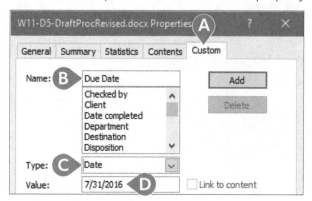

Ⓐ Click the **Custom** tab.

Ⓑ Type **Due Date** in the Name field.

Ⓒ Select **Date** from the Type list.

Ⓓ Type **7/31/2016** in the Value field and then click **OK**.

Remember, custom properties do not appear in the Properties panel in Backstage view. Refer to the Custom tab in the Advanced Properties dialog box to view custom properties.

4. Save and close the document.

Automating Tasks with Macros

Macros are useful for automating routine tasks, especially those that involve many steps. You can record a series of steps using the macro recorder, and then play them back automatically when needed. For example, you may need to switch to a color printer frequently. You can record the steps of the process in a macro, and, when it's time to switch printers, the macro can quickly perform the steps. Whenever you find yourself doing the same thing over and over, you have a candidate for a macro.

☰ View→Macros→Macros

Assign Macros to a Toolbar or a Keyboard Shortcut

If you intend to use a macro frequently, you can assign it to a keyboard shortcut or a button on the Quick Access toolbar for easy access. This is not required, though. You can always run a macro directly from the Macros dialog box.

Store Macros

Macros can be stored in documents or templates, including the Normal.dotm template, which is the default. The *m* in the *.dotm* file extension indicates the template can contain macros. Macros stored there are available to all documents on the system.

Macro names cannot contain spaces. —

You can assign a macro to run from a Quick Access toolbar button or a keyboard shortcut. —

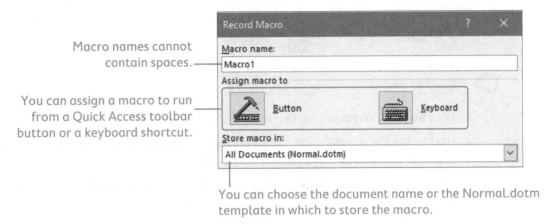

You can choose the document name or the Normal.dotm template in which to store the macro.

Recording Limitations

Certain mouse motions such as scrolling, selecting options from drop-down lists, and resizing windows cannot be recorded in macros. You may also find that certain commands are grayed out on the Ribbon or in the drop-down list during the macro recording. You can overcome these limitations by choosing alternative techniques. For example, if selecting an item from a drop-down list doesn't record in a macro, display the dialog box containing the feature and make the selection there. Instead of scrolling in a document, use arrow keys to position the insertion point (keystrokes are recorded). Likewise, when selecting text with the mouse fails to record, try [Shift] plus arrow keys or other keyboard shortcuts.

When you record a macro and change settings in a dialog box using arrow keys, the change normally sticks until you exit Word; this means the dialog box doesn't reset to its default state. As a result, running the macro again in the same session may change the setting to the *next* option in the dialog box.

 When necessary, reset the dialog box to the default state as part of the macro.

DEVELOP YOUR SKILLS: W11-D7

In this exercise, you will record a macro that sets up the orientation, margins, and page size for a survey form. The macro will also insert and format text.

1. Create a new, blank document.
2. Choose **View→Macros→Macros** 🖩 **menu button** ▼ **→Record Macro**.

3. Follow these steps to name the macro and begin the recording process:

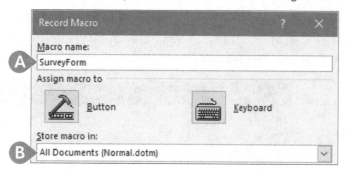

- Ⓐ Type **SurveyForm** (no spaces) in the Macro Name field.
- Ⓑ Ensure that the storage location is the **Normal.dotm** template, which makes the macro available to all documents on your computer; click **OK**.

The mouse pointer now has a cassette tape attached to it, indicating that your steps are being recorded. Now you will perform the steps you wish to record.

4. Choose **Home→Styles** and click the **No Spacing** style in the Quick Styles gallery.

This sets line spacing at 1.0 and removes the after-paragraph spacing.

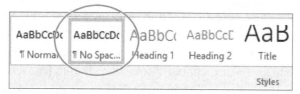

5. Choose **Home→Font→Bold** `B`.

6. Type **Raritan Clinic East Pediatric Diagnostic Specialties**.

7. Choose **Layout→Page Setup→Orientation** 🗗 and then choose **Landscape**.

8. Choose **Layout→Page Setup→Margins** ▦ and then choose **Custom Margins** at the bottom of the gallery.

9. Set the top and bottom margins to **0.4"** and the left and right margins to **0.5"**.

10. Click the **Paper** tab at the top of the dialog box and set the width to **7"** and the height to **5"**.

11. Click **OK** to apply the settings.

Stop Recording and Run the Macro

12. Choose **View→Macros→Macros** 🔲 **menu button** ▾ **→Stop Recording**.

The macro is now ready for playback.

13. Close the document without saving it and then create a new, blank document.

14. Choose **View→Macros→Macros** 🔲.

15. Follow these steps to run the macro:

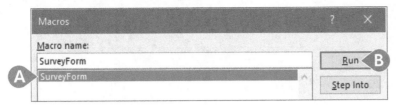

ⓐ Choose your **SurveyForm** macro.

ⓑ Click **Run**.

Your macro should create a copy of your survey form. The heading line is selected. You can click to deselect. If you made an error in the macro, you could delete the incorrect macro and record it again. Later in the chapter, you will learn to make minor edits in the VBA Editor.

16. Close the document without saving it and then create a new, blank document.

Editing Macros with the VBA Editor

Visual Basic for Applications (VBA) is a macro programming language that runs in Office 2016 applications. When you record a macro, you are creating a Visual Basic module containing program instructions that execute when you run the macro. This topic provides a brief introduction to Visual Basic, but a complete discussion is beyond the scope of this course.

You can edit a macro by displaying the Visual Basic module and modifying the code. The editor has its own menus, toolbars, and commands, which allow you to develop, edit, and test Visual Basic applications.

DEVELOP YOUR SKILLS: W11-D8

In this exercise, you will open the Visual Basic editor and revise your macro. Then you will run the modified macro.

1. Choose **View→Macros→Macros** 🔳.

2. Follow these steps to begin the editing process:

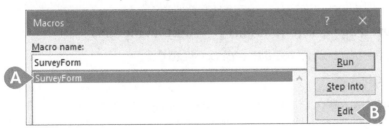

ⓐ Choose your **SurveyForm** macro.

ⓑ Click **Edit**.

3. Follow these steps to modify the code:

```
Normal - NewMacros (Code)

(General)

    Sub SurveyForm()
    '
    '  SurveyForm Macro
    '
    '
        Selection.Style = ActiveDocument.Styles("No Spacing")
        Selection.Font.Bold = wdToggle
        Selection.TypeText Text:= _
            "Raritan Clinic East Pediatric Diagnostic Specialties"   Ⓐ
        If Selection.PageSetup.Orientation = wdOrientPortrait Then
            Selection.PageSetup.Orientation = wdOrientLandscape
        Else
            Selection.PageSetup.Orientation = wdOrientPortrait
        End If
        Selection.WholeStory
        With ActiveDocument.Styles(wdStyleNormal).Font
            If .NameFarEast = .NameAscii Then
                .NameAscii = ""
            End If
            .NameFarEast = ""
        End With
        With ActiveDocument.PageSetup
            .LineNumbering.Active = False
            .Orientation = wdOrientLandscape
            .TopMargin = InchesToPoints(0.4)
            .BottomMargin = InchesToPoints(0.4)       Ⓑ
            .LeftMargin = InchesToPoints(0.5)
            .RightMargin = InchesToPoints(0.5)
            .Gutter = InchesToPoints(0)
```

Ⓐ Change the word *Specialties* to **Specialists**.

Ⓑ Change the TopMargin and BottomMargin settings from 0.4 to **0.5**.

4. Choose **File→Close and Return to Microsoft Word**.

The changes are saved automatically. Now you will test the edited macro.

5. Choose **View→Macros→Macros** 📧, choose **SurveyForm** in the Macro Name list, and then click **Run**.

Notice that the word Specialties was changed to Specialists.

6. Choose **Layout→Page Setup→Margins** 📧**→Custom Margins**.

Notice that the top and bottom margins are now set to 0.5.

7. Close the dialog box.

8. Close the document without saving; create a new, blank document.

Running Macros from the Quick Access Toolbar

When you create a macro to automate repetitive tasks, you are trying to increase efficiency. To make macros run more efficiently, you can assign them to a button on the Quick Access toolbar or to a shortcut keystroke. By taking advantage of these time-saving tools, you alleviate the tedious nature of displaying the Macros dialog box and selecting the macro each time you want to run it.

You can assign a toolbar button or keyboard shortcut to a macro as you record it. In addition, you can assign a toolbar button to an existing macro using the Quick Access toolbar commands in the Word Options dialog box. Word offers numerous button images that you can choose to help keep your macro buttons straight.

 View the video "Assign a Macro to the Quick Access Toolbar."

DEVELOP YOUR SKILLS: W11-D9

In this exercise, you will assign the SurveyForm macro to a Quick Access toolbar button.

1. Choose **File→Options** and then click the **Quick Access Toolbar** category.

2. Follow these steps to assign a macro button to the Quick Access toolbar:

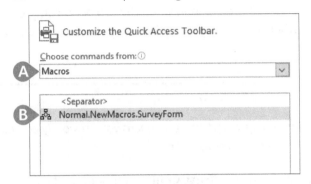 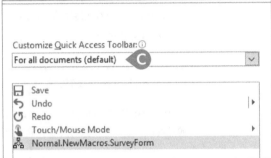

Ⓐ Choose **Macros** here.

Ⓑ Select the **SurveyForm** macro.

Ⓒ Ensure that **For All Documents (Default)** appears here.

3. Click the **Add** button in the middle of the dialog box to add the macro to the Quick Access Toolbar list and then click **OK**.

Notice that a new button appears on the Quick Access toolbar.

4. Hover the mouse pointer over the button to see the button name in a ToolTip; click the button to run the macro.

Leave the document open.

Macro Security

Macro attacks were more prevalent in earlier versions of Microsoft Office. Added security features in recent versions have caused virus creators to pursue other avenues; however, it's always better to be safe than sorry. The Trust Center in the Word Options dialog box contains security settings.

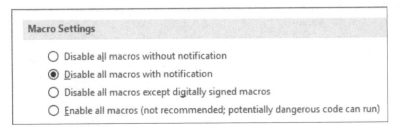

MACRO SETTINGS OPTIONS

Option	What It Does
Disable all macros without notification	Word disables all macros and does not notify users.
Disable all macros with notification	This is the default setting. It gives the user the option to enable or disable a macro.
Disable all macros except digitally signed macros	This option allows users to enable or disable only digitally signed macros.
Enable all macros (not recommended; potentially dangerous code can run)	This option significantly reduces security and could potentially cause serious damage.

Deleting Macros

You may create a macro for use in a special project, and when the project is complete you no longer need the macro. Deleting a macro when it's no longer required helps keep the list of macros from becoming unwieldy.

DEVELOP YOUR SKILLS: W11-D10

In this exercise, you will review security settings and delete the macro you previously created. Finally, you will remove the macro button from the Quick Access toolbar.

1. Choose **File→Options** and then choose the **Trust Center** category on the left.
2. Click the **Trust Center Settings** button and review the Macro Settings options at the top of the dialog box.

   You will not make any changes to security settings.

3. Click **Cancel** twice to close the dialog boxes.

   Now you will delete your macro.

4. Choose **View→Macros→Macros** .
5. Choose the **SurveyForm** macro in the Macro Name list, click **Delete**, click **Yes** to verify the deletion, and then close the dialog box.

   Now you will remove the macro button from the Quick Access toolbar.

6. Right-click the macro button and choose **Remove from Quick Access Toolbar**.
7. Exit Word without saving the document.

Self-Assessment

Check your knowledge of this chapter's key concepts and skills using the Self-Assessment in your ebook or eLab course.

Reinforce Your Skills

REINFORCE YOUR SKILLS: W11-R1

Streamline Kids for Change Office Procedures

Kids for Change is streamlining its office procedures. Staff members will review various options to determine which changes will help them be more efficient. In this exercise, you will prepare screenshots of the features you would like staff members to consider for personalizing Word.

Before You Begin: *Be prepared to take notes of changes you make to settings so you can reset the options later if necessary.*

1. Start Word, open **W11-R1-WordOptions** from your **Word Chapter 11** folder, and save it as **W11-R1-WordOptionsRevised**.

   First, you will create an AutoCorrect shortcut for a Kids for Change Nature Hikes project.

2. Choose **File→Options→Proofing** and click the **AutoCorrect Options** button.

3. Type **kfcnh** in the Replace field, type **Kids for Change Nature Hikes** in the With field, and click **OK** twice.

4. Position the insertion point at the end of the document; then type **AutoCorrect Shortcut: kfcnh** and tap [Enter].

   Now you will work with Save options.

5. Choose **File→Options,** choose the **Save** category, and change the AutoRecover interval to **15** minutes.

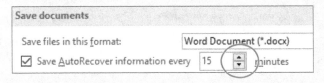

6. Check the **Save to Computer by Default** checkbox.

7. Click the **Browse** button to the right of the Default Local File Location field.

8. In the Modify Location dialog box, navigate to the **Desktop** and click **OK**.

   Now you will take a screenshot of the Word Options dialog box and paste it into your Word Options document.

9. Press [Alt]+[PrtScn] to take a screenshot of the dialog box and then click **OK** to close the dialog box.

10. Press [Ctrl]+[V] to paste the screenshot and then resize the screenshot to about a third of the original size.

11. Create a new, blank document so you can test the default local file location.

12. Choose **File→Save As** and click **Browse** at the bottom of the left-hand panel.

    Notice that the path at the top of the dialog box leads to the Desktop. The change worked.

13. Click **Cancel** to close the Save As dialog box.

14. Click **Close** in the far-left panel to close the blank document without saving it.

Customize the Recent Documents List

15. Choose **File→Options→Advanced** category.

16. Scroll down to the **Display** options and change the number of recent documents to **8**.

17. Press Alt + PrtScn to take a screenshot and click **OK**.

18. Ensure the insertion point is at the end of the document, tap Enter, and paste the screenshot into your document, resizing the screenshot to about a third of the original size.

19. If necessary, resize the screenshots until they both fit on the first page of the document.

20. Choose **File→Open** and notice that a maximum of eight documents appear in the Recent Documents list.

Now you will pin a document to the Recent Documents list.

21. Hover the mouse pointer over a filename to display the pushpin icon at the right and then click the pushpin to pin the document to the list.

The document will remain in the list until it is unpinned.

22. Right-click the document you just pinned and choose **Unpin from List**.

You can clear all documents, except pinned documents, from the list.

23. Right-click any document in the Recent Documents list and notice (but don't click) the Clear Unpinned Documents command.

24. Tap Esc to close the menu.

Now you will restore the settings you changed in the Word Options dialog box.

25. Retrieve the list of changes that you noted earlier and, if necessary, restore the following options to their original settings:
- AutoRecover interval
- Save to Computer by Default checkbox
- Default Local File Location path
- Number of Recent Documents displayed

Create a Custom Property

26. Choose **File→Info**, click the **Properties** button at the top of the Properties panel, and click **Advanced Properties**.

27. Click the **Custom** tab and follow these guidelines to create a custom property:
- Choose **Checked By** from the Name list.
- Leave the data type at **Text**.
- Type **Reviewer Sean Oct 17** in the Value field.

You have requested that each reviewer sign in here so you can easily track who has already reviewed the document and when.

28. Take a screenshot of the dialog box, click **OK**, and then click **Back** ⬅.

29. Make sure the insertion point is at the end of the document.

30. Tap [Enter] and paste the screenshot in your Word Options document and resize to about a third of its original size.

This screenshot will appear on page 2.

31. Save and close the file.

Create Kids for Change Carbon Footprint Macro

Kids for Change operates on a tight budget, so it types its own document header information manually. The group is currently working on a carbon footprint project and wants that information to appear in the headers of documents related to the project. Because this is something it will do over and over, it knows it has a good candidate for a macro. In this exercise, you will create and test the macro.

1. Create a new, blank document.

2. Choose **View→Macros→Macros** 🖼 **menu button ▾→Record Macro**.

3. Name the macro **Header** and verify that the **Normal** template is chosen in the Store Macro In field.

4. Click **OK** to start recording.

The mouse pointer now has a cassette tape attached to it indicating that your steps are being recorded.

5. Choose **Insert→Header & Footer→Header** 📄 and then choose **Edit Header** at the bottom of the gallery.

6. Tap [Tab] to position the insertion point in the center of the header and type **Kids for Change**.

You can't double-click in the document body to close the header area. This is one of those mouse movements that the macro recorder can't record.

7. Choose **Header & Footer Tools→Design→Close→Close Header and Footer** ⊗.

8. Choose **View→Macros→Macros menu button ▾→Stop Recording**.

9. Close the document without saving; start a new, blank document.

Now you will run the macro.

10. Choose **View→Macros→Macros**, make sure the Header macro is chosen, and then click **Run** and observe the header.

11. Close the document without saving; start a new, blank document.

Use the VBA Editor to Modify the Macro

12. Choose **View→Macros→Macros**, verify that the **Header** macro is chosen, click **Edit**, and then locate the Kids for Change text.

```
End If
ActiveWindow.ActivePane.View.SeekView = wdSeekCurrentPageHeader
Selection.TypeText Text:=vbTab & "Kids for Change"
ActiveWindow.ActivePane.View.SeekView = wdSeekMainDocument
```

13. Position the insertion point to the right of the word *Change*, tap [Spacebar], and type **Carbon Footprint Project**.

14. Choose **File→Close** and Return to Microsoft Word.

Now you will assign the macro to a keyboard shortcut and run the macro to verify your editing changes.

Assign the Macro to a Keyboard Shortcut

15. Choose **File→Options** and choose the **Customize Ribbon** category.

Notice the Customize button next to Keyboard Shortcuts at the bottom of the left-hand panel.

Keyboard shortcuts: Customize...

16. Click **Customize**; scroll down and choose **Macros** from the Categories list on the left.

17. Choose the **Header** macro in the field on the right.

18. Position the insertion point in the **Press New Shortcut Key** field and press [Ctrl]+[9].

Below the Current Keys field at left, notice that the shortcut you entered is currently unassigned.

19. Click the **Assign** button to assign the shortcut to your macro, click **Close**, and then click **OK**.

Now you will test the macro.

20. Press [Ctrl]+[9] to run the macro and notice the editing change you made.

Review Macro Security and Delete the Macro

21. Choose **File→Options→Trust Center**, click the **Trust Center Settings** button, and review the Macro Settings at the top of the dialog box.

You will not change any security settings.

22. Click **Cancel** twice to close the dialog boxes.

23. Choose **View→Macros→Macros** 🖾, verify that the **Header** macro is chosen, and then click **Delete**.

24. Click **Yes** to confirm the deletion and then close the Macros dialog box.

25. Save the file as **W11-R2-Header** in your **Word Chapter 11 folder** and then close it.

REINFORCE YOUR SKILLS: W11-R3

Personalize Options and Create a Tutoring Schedule Macro

Kids for Change will participate in an after-school tutoring program. In this exercise, you will personalize Word to work more efficiently and create a macro that generates a table where you can set up the weekly tutoring schedule.

Before You Begin: *Be prepared to take notes of changes you make to settings, so you can reset the options later if necessary.*

1. Open **W11-R3-Tutoring** from your **Word Chapter 11** folder and save it as **W11-R3-TutoringRevised**.

2. Choose **File→Options→Save** and change the AutoRecover interval to **5** minutes.

3. Check the **Save to Computer by Default** checkbox.

4. Click the **Browse** button to the right of the Default Local File Location field, navigate to the **Desktop**, and then click **OK** twice.

Now you will observe the change to the default file location.

5. Start a new, blank document.

Remember, you saved the tutoring file outside of the default location; therefore, if you click Browse, you will access its original storage location. You will use the new, blank document to test the storage location you just set.

6. Choose **File→Save As** and note that *This PC* is highlighted.

7. Click the **Browse** button and notice that the path at the top of the Save As dialog box leads to the Desktop.

8. Click **Cancel** to close the Save As dialog box and then choose **Close** on the left to close the blank document without saving it.

Pin a Document to the Recent Documents List

9. Choose **File→Open**, hover the mouse pointer over a filename, and notice the pushpin icon to its right.

10. Click the pushpin to move the file into the Pinned category at the top of the list.

11. Click the pushpin again to unpin the document and return it to the main list.

Now you will restore the default settings that you noted earlier.

12. Click **Options** on the left and restore the following items to their original settings:
    - AutoRecover interval
    - Save to Computer by Default
    - Default Local File Location

Record and Run a Macro

Now you will create a table macro that Kids for Change can use each week to set up the tutoring schedule.

13. Position the insertion point at the end of the Tutoring document.

14. Choose **View→Macros→Macros** 📑 **menu button ▾→Record Macro**.

15. Name the macro **TutorTable** and verify that the **Normal** template is chosen in the Store Macro In field.

Now you will assign the macro to a keyboard shortcut.

16. Click the **Keyboard** button.

17. Ensure that Macros appears in the left column and then choose the **TutorTable** macro on the right.

18. Position the insertion point in the **Press New Shortcut Key** field and press ⎡Ctrl⎤+⎡8⎤.

Notice that the shortcut is unassigned.

19. Click **Assign** and then click **Close**.

20. Choose **Insert→Tables→Table** ▦ and drag in the grid to create a **5x7** table.

The insertion point should be in the first table cell. Macro recording limitations do not allow you to drag the mouse pointer to select cells, so you will need to use keystrokes instead.

21. Press ⎡Shift⎤ and tap ⎡→⎤ 5 times to select the first row.

22. Choose **Table Tools→Layout→Merge→Merge Cells** ▥.

23. Choose **Table Tools→Layout→Alignment→Align Center** ▣ and type **Weekly Tutoring Schedule**.

24. Enter the remaining text shown, using arrow keys to position the insertion point.

Remember, macro recording limitations don't allow you to position the insertion point with the mouse pointer.

Weekly Tutoring Schedule				
	Max	Allison	Manuel	Margarita
Monday				
Tuesday				
Wednesday				
Thursday				
Friday				

25. Choose **View→Macros→Macros** 🔳 **menu button ▾ →Stop Recording**.

Now you will remove the table so you can recreate it with the macro. Nelly is replacing Allison while she is out of town, so you'll make that change to the macro first.

26. Select the table, right-click the table, and choose **Delete Table** from the pop-up menu.

27. Choose **View→Macros→Macros** 🔳, make sure the **TutorTable** macro is chosen, and then click **Edit**.

28. Locate Allison's name. (You may need to enlarge the Visual Basic window—Allison is near the bottom.)

```
End With
Selection.MoveRight Unit:=wdCharacter, Count:=5, Extend:=wdExtend
Selection.Cells.Merge
Selection.SelectCell
Selection.ParagraphFormat.Alignment = wdAlignParagraphCenter
Selection.Cells.VerticalAlignment = wdCellAlignVerticalCenter
Selection.TypeText Text:="Weekly Tutoring ScheduleMax"
Selection.MoveRight Unit:=wdCell
Selection.TypeText Text:="Allison"
```

29. Double-click *Allison* to select it and type **Nelly**.

30. Choose **File→Close** and Return to Microsoft Word.

Now you will run the macro to see your editing changes.

31. Click in the last blank line on the page and then press ⌨Ctrl+⌨8 to run the macro.

Notice Nelly's name in the table. Now you will delete the macro.

32. Choose **View→Macros→Macros** 🔳.

33. Make sure the **TutorTable** macro is selected, click **Delete**, and click **Yes** when the message appears confirming the deletion.

34. Close the Macros dialog box and save and close the file.

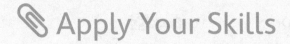 Apply Your Skills

APPLY YOUR SKILLS: W11-A1

Review Office Efficiency

The Universal Corporate Events office manager is reviewing various options to determine whether it is possible to make work more efficient for the company. In this exercise, you will create an AutoCorrect shortcut, change options for saving, and work with document properties.

Before You Begin: *Be prepared to take notes of changes you make to settings, so you can reset the options later if necessary.*

1. Open **W11-A1-Efficiency** from your **Word Chapter 11** folder and save it as **W11-A1-EfficiencyRevised**.

2. Open the **Word Options** dialog box, choose the **Proofing** category, and click the **AutoCorrect Options** button.

   Creating a shortcut for the company name will certainly be a time-saver.

3. Enter **uce** in the Replace field and **Universal Corporate Events** in the With field; click **OK** twice.

4. Position the insertion point at the bottom of the document and type **uce** ⌷Enter⌷ to test the shortcut.

5. Open the **Word Options** dialog box; in the **Save** category, change the **AutoRecover** interval to **30** minutes.

6. Check the **Save to Computer by Default** checkbox.

7. Use the **Browse** button to the right of the Default Local File Location and set the path to the **Desktop**.

8. Take a screenshot (⌷Alt⌷+⌷PrtScn⌷) of the **Word Options** dialog box, paste it at the end of your document, and resize it to about a third of its original size.

9. Create a new, blank document and choose **File→Save As**.

10. Click the **Browse** button to test your default file location (Desktop) and then cancel the dialog box and close the blank document.

    Now you will restore the default settings.

11. Retrieve your list of default settings you wrote down earlier and reset the defaults in the Word Options dialog box.

12. In the Properties panel in Backstage view, type **Efficiency** in the Tags field.

13. Use the **Properties** button to open the **Advanced Properties** dialog box.

14. Follow these guidelines to add a custom property:
    - Property Name: **Checked By**
    - Property Type: **Text**
    - Property Value: **Matt Robinson**

    As staff members review the potential procedural changes, they will enter their names in the Properties dialog box so you can tell when everyone has completed the review.

15. Take a screenshot of the **Custom** tab, click **OK**, and then click **Back** ⬅.

16. Position the insertion point at the end of the document, generate a blank line, and paste the screenshot, resizing it to about a third of its original size.

17. Save and close the file.

APPLY YOUR SKILLS: W11-A2

Create a Las Vegas Macro

Universal Corporate Events is preparing a Las Vegas tour for a corporate client. As agents are communicating via email with the travelers, they will paste the macro text into the email as needed. In this exercise, you will create and edit the macro and run it from the Quick Access toolbar.

1. Open **W11-A2-LasVegasMacro** from your **Word Chapter 11** folder and save it as **W11-A2-LasVegasMacroRevised**.

2. Start a new, blank document and then start the macro recorder.

3. Name the macro **LasVegas**, verify the **Normal** template is chosen, and then click **OK**.

4. Record this text in the blank document:

   Upon arrival at the airport, pick up your bags in the luggage area and then look for a limousine driver with a Silicon Tech Group sign. The driver will take you to the MGM Grand where you will stay during your visit.

5. Stop the macro recorder, tap [Enter], and then test your macro to ensure it runs as expected.

   Now you will edit the macro and assign it to a toolbar button.

6. Open the macro editor and locate the word *airport* in the VBA code.

7. Position the insertion point in front of *airport*, type **Las Vegas**, and then tap [Spacebar].

8. Close the macro editor and then open the **Word Options** dialog box.

9. Choose the **Quick Access Toolbar** category and choose **Macros** from the commands list.

10. Add your macro to the list on the right and then click the **Modify** button.

11. Choose the envelope button, change the **Display Name** to **Las Vegas**, and click **OK** twice.

12. Tap [Enter] and then run the macro from the Quick Access toolbar and verify your editing change.

13. Take a screenshot of the document you used to run your macro and then switch to **W11-A2-LasVegasMacroRevised**.

14. Position the insertion point at the bottom of the document and then paste the screenshot.

15. Delete the macro and remove the macro button from the Quick Access toolbar.

16. Save and close the file and close the other document without saving it.

APPLY YOUR SKILLS: W11-A3

Get Ready for the Corporate Trainer

Universal Corporate Events staff will have an opportunity to review some advanced Word features with the corporate trainer. The staff will practice with some of the features and note questions they have for the trainer. In this exercise, you will work with an AutoCorrect shortcut and the Word Options dialog box, and you will create and edit a macro.

Before You Begin: *Be prepared to take notes of changes you make to settings, so you can reset the options later if necessary.*

1. Open **W11-A3-BrownBag** from your **Word Chapter 11** folder and save it as **W11-A3-BrownBagRevised**.

   First you will create an AutoCorrect shortcut. You will soon be making travel arrangements for a new client, Morgan, Alexander, and Swift, and you will type the client name many times, so a shortcut will be a real time-saver.

2. Open the **Word Options** dialog box, choose the **Proofing** category, and click the **AutoCorrect Options** button.

3. Enter **mas** in the Replace field and **Morgan, Alexander, and Swift** in the With field; click **OK** twice.

4. Position the insertion point at the end of your document, type **mas**, and tap ⌷Enter⌷ to test the shortcut.

5. Open the **Word Options** dialog box, choose the **Save** category, and change the **AutoRecover** interval to **20** minutes.

6. Check the **Save to Computer by Default** checkbox.

7. Use the **Browse** button to change the default local file location to the **Desktop**.

8. Take a screenshot of the **Word Options** dialog box, click **OK**, paste it at the end of your document, and resize it to about a third of its original size.

9. Create a new, blank document so you can test your changes.

10. In the **Backstage, Save As** screen, click **Browse** and check that the path at the top of the Save As dialog box targets the **Desktop**.

11. Click **Cancel** to close the Save As dialog box and close the blank document without saving.

12. Restore the default settings in the Word Options dialog box.

Create, Run, and Edit a Macro

Now you will create a macro that you will use with another client whose employees will visit the Van Gogh Museum in Amsterdam. There is information that will be used in many letters, so it's a good candidate for a macro.

13. Position the insertion point at the end of your document and generate a blank line.

14. Turn on the macro recorder, name the macro **VanGogh**, and ensure the **Normal** template is chosen.

15. Click the **Keyboard** button and assign ⌷Ctrl⌷+⌷7⌷ to the macro.

16. Record the following text:

```
The Van Gogh Museum is open daily from 9 am to 5 pm. It is
located at Amstel 51, Amsterdam, and you can get there by boat
shuttle or the Hop on, Hop off bus.
```

17. Turn off the macro recorder and tap [Enter] to generate a blank line.

18. Use [Ctrl]+[7] to test the macro.

Now you will enter additional information in the macro.

19. Open the macro editor and locate the word *bus* at the end of the macro text.

20. Position the insertion point after the period following the word *bus* and tap [Spacebar].

21. Add the following text and then close the macro editor:

```
Be sure to see The Potato Eaters and Starry Night.
```

22. Tap [Enter] and test the macro to verify your change and then delete the macro.

23. Save and close the file.

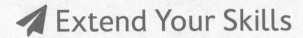

Extend Your Skills

These exercises challenge you to think critically and apply your new skills. You will be evaluated on your ability to follow directions, completeness, creativity, and the use of proper grammar and mechanics. Save files to your chapter folder. Submit assignments as directed.

W11-E1 That's the Way I See It

As the owner of a small business, you know it's important for your staff to operate as efficiently as possible. You're a whiz with Word, and you want to show your employees some features that can help them effectively organize the Word environment. Write a one- to two-page document explaining how the following might help them:

▸ When would it be beneficial to change the AutoRecover time interval?

▸ Under what circumstances would changing the default file location be helpful?

▸ What is the benefit of pinning documents to the Recent Document list?

▸ How can custom properties be useful?

Add two or three screenshots to help make your concepts come alive. Add your own Title and Comment to the Properties panel in Backstage view for the document you create. Save your file as **W11-E1-WordIdeas**.

W11-E2 Be Your Own Boss

As an administrator at Blue Jean Landscaping, you have found that macros can greatly increase efficiency. You want to create a macro that will rapidly create a letterhead, with the added benefit of avoiding printing costs. Create a new document named **W11-E2-BJLetterhead**. Record a new **Letterhead** macro and store it in the Normal template.

Type **Blue Jean Landscaping** as the company name and make up the rest of the letterhead content. Delete the text you used to create the macro and then test it. Delete the letterhead text and then edit the macro to add a comma, Spacebar , and **Inc.** at the end of the company name. Test the macro again; if it runs as intended, save the document.

W11-E3 Demonstrate Proficiency

The owner of Stormy BBQ just attended a Microsoft Word class at the local community college, and it opened his eyes to some of the beneficial features that he had not been aware of. Knowing that you are a very experienced Word user, he has asked you to record some ideas about how Word options and macros can benefit the business. Write a one- to two-page paper explaining what Word options (at least three) you would modify and why. Also, think of three different types of Word documents you use at Stormy BBQ and suggest at least one macro for each document type that would make creating the document more efficient. Don't forget to explain why. Use the Properties panel to add a Title and Tag. Save your file as **W11-E3-EfficientStormy**.

12 | Integrating Word with Excel, PowerPoint, and the Web

One advantage to using a suite of applications is that they are designed to share data and information and to work together seamlessly. You can display data stored in an Excel worksheet in a Word document or use Excel data as the source document in Mail Merge. You can send a Word outline to PowerPoint to create a new presentation or insert a PowerPoint presentation in a Word document. You can open a PDF file in Word and edit it, and you can convert a Word document to a web page. In this chapter, you will explore the features that allow Word to interact with other Office programs.

LEARNING OBJECTIVES

▸ Embed and link Excel objects in Word

▸ Use an Excel worksheet as a Mail Merge data file

▸ Create PowerPoint presentations from Word outlines

▸ Insert PowerPoint presentations in Word documents

▸ Open a PDF file in Word for editing

▸ Convert Word documents to web pages

📁 Project: Multitasking with Word, Excel, and PowerPoint

You are an administrative assistant at Raritan Clinic East. An advisory committee meets quarterly to review the budget and clinic activities. In preparation for the upcoming meeting, you will help create the quarterly expense report. The data is in an Excel worksheet, so you will use the Excel data in the report that you will prepare in Word. You will add the chart contained in the Excel file to the report and prepare a PowerPoint presentation using an outline of headings from the clinic's Annual Report. You will generate a letter to all committee members using an Excel name and address file to address the letters. Then you will edit a press release in Word that was saved in PDF format. Finally, you will save your report as a web page for posting on the clinic website for others to review.

Embedding and Linking Excel Objects

You can share data and objects among the programs in the Office 2016 suite. Object is a term for an element that you share between files. For example, you can place data and chart objects from an Excel file in a Word document. You would choose to embed an object if you don't want it to change when the original source file is updated. On the other hand, if you want the Word document to stay current with any changes in the source file, you would link the object to its original file so your document will be updated when the source file is modified.

Link or Embed Data

Whether you are embedding or linking to files, there are two techniques for inserting data from other files:

▶ **Copy/Paste:** Using this procedure, you copy data from a source document, such as an Excel worksheet, and paste it directly into the Word document. Using the Paste Special command, you can choose to link the data or not at the time you paste it. This method is useful when you want to include only a portion of the file.

▶ **Insert Object:** You can insert a file, such as an Excel workbook, from within Word, and you can choose to link the data or not at the time you insert it. This procedure is useful when you want to include an entire file in a document.

DEVELOP YOUR SKILLS: W12-D1

In this exercise, you will embed an Excel worksheet in a Word document and test its static nature.

1. Start Word; create a new, blank document; and save it to your **Word Chapter 12** folder as **W12-D1-BudgetRpt**.

2. Type these heading lines:

   Advisory Committee Budget Report
   Third Quarter 2016

3. Tap [Enter] and then select both heading lines.

4. Choose **Home→Styles→More** ⊡ on the Quick Styles gallery and choose the **Title** style.

5. Position the insertion point in the blank line below the heading lines and type this introductory paragraph:

This report, produced by clinic staff, is in keeping with the Advisory Committee's decision to conduct quarterly reviews of the current year's budget. It provides a snapshot of expenses for the quarter and for the year-to-date.

6. Tap Enter and then choose **Insert→Text→Object**.

7. Follow these steps to identify the Excel file from which to embed the data:

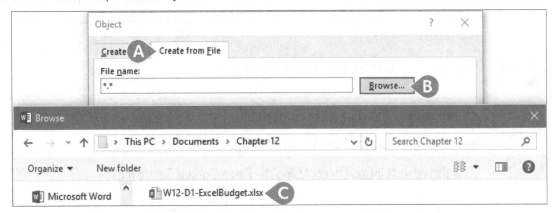

Ⓐ Click the **Create from File** tab.

Ⓑ Click the **Browse** button and navigate to your **Word Chapter 12** folder.

Ⓒ Double-click **W12-D1-ExcelBudget** and click **OK**.

Modify the Source File

8. Start Excel, open **W12-D1-ExcelBudget**, and save it in your **Word Chapter 12** folder as **W12-D1-ExcelBudgetRevised**.

9. Follow these steps to edit a value in the source file:

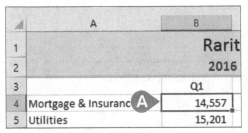 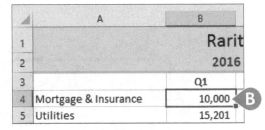

Ⓐ Click the cell for **14,557** (Q1, Mortgage & Insurance) and tap Delete.

Ⓑ Type **10,000** and tap Enter.

10. Switch to Word and verify that the value of Q1 Mortgagee & Insurance remains 14,557.

Because the table is embedded (not linked) in the document, the data in Word is not affected by changes made to the Excel file.

11. Switch back to Excel and click **Undo** ↺ twice to return the value to its original amount.

Because you actually want the report to reflect the most recent data in the worksheet, you will delete the embedded object and then link to the data in the next exercise.

12. Switch back to Word, click the embedded worksheet to select it, and tap Delete.

13. Save the Word file and leave all files open.

Link Objects

When you link data from another application, such as Excel or PowerPoint, to a Word document, the original information resides in Excel or PowerPoint. This is known as the source file because it is the source of the data. When you place the information (object) in a Word document, it becomes the destination file. By linking source files with Word documents, you create a dynamic tie between the two files.

For example, you might start working on a quarterly report before the end of the quarter, and, if there is a linked chart in the report, it updates with the current information as the numbers change in Excel. That way, updates are centralized, and you don't have to keep track of making changes in two places.

 Note! *Moving or renaming the source file breaks the link.*

 View the video "Inserting a Linked Object."

 View the video "Link an Object with Paste Special."

 View the video "Link an Object Using the Paste Options Smart Tag."

≡ Insert→Text→Object→Create from File→Link to File

DEVELOP YOUR SKILLS: W12-D2

In this exercise, you will link Excel data to a Word document using Paste Special. You will then modify the Excel worksheet and observe how the changes update the Word document. Then you will link an Excel chart to the document using the Paste Options smart tag.

1. Save your file as **W12-D2-BudgetRpt**.

2. Switch to Excel and follow these steps to select and copy the Excel data:

A1	▼	× ✓ *fx*	Raritan Clinic East		

	A	B	C	D	E	F
1			Raritan Clinic East		Ⓐ	
2			2014 Budget Summary			
3		Q1	Q2	Q3	Q4	Totals
4	Mortgage & Insurance	14,557	14,557	14,557		43,671
5	Utilities	15,201	18,200	21,000		54,401
6	Food	5,480	4,512	3,452		13,444
7	Staff Salaries	87,685	87,685	87,685		263,055
8	Maintenance & Repairs	16,982	17,458	15,225		49,665
9	Fundraising for Donations	820	2,006	67,325		70,151
10	Grand Totals	140,725	144,418	209,244	-	494,387	Ⓑ

Ⓒ

Ⓐ Click in the merged cell containing the heading *Raritan Clinic East*.

Ⓑ Press [Shift] and click the last cell in the worksheet, **494,387**.

Ⓒ Choose **Home→Clipboard→Copy**.

3. Switch to Word and position the insertion point at the end of the document.

4. Choose **Home→Clipboard→Paste** 📋 **menu button** ▾**→Paste Special**.

5. When the Paste Special dialog box opens, follow these steps to paste the object:

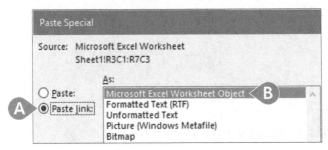

Ⓐ Choose **Paste Link**.

Ⓑ Choose **Microsoft Excel Worksheet Object** and click **OK**.

Now you will edit the worksheet and observe the change to the linked object in Word.

6. Switch to Excel and tap ⌷Esc⌷ to remove the marquee (animated dashed line) surrounding the table.

The marquee in Excel identifies the cells copied.

7. Click **cell E4**, which is the Q4 cell for Mortgage & Insurance.

8. Type the Q4 projections shown, tapping ⌷Enter⌷ after typing each number.

The formulas in the Totals cells automatically update as you enter the data.

Q4
11,337
1,750
4,975
17,685
2,543
1,529

9. Switch to Word.

The linked table updated with the additions you made in the Q4 column. If the Excel table failed to update on your computer, right-click the Excel object and choose Update Link.

10. Position the insertion point at the end of the document and tap ⌷Enter⌷ three times.

Link an Excel Chart in Word

Now you will use the Paste Options smart tag to link a chart to Word.

11. Switch to Excel, click the **Sheet 2** tab at the bottom of the Excel window, and click the pie chart border once to select it.

The mouse pointer becomes a four-headed arrow, and the selection handles appear in the border.

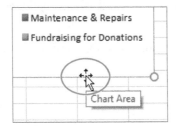

12. Choose **Home→Clipboard→Copy** 📋 and then switch back to Word.

13. Choose **Home→Clipboard→Paste** 📋.

14. Follow these steps to paste a link for the chart object:

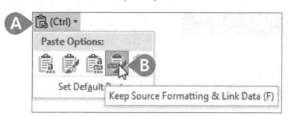

Ⓐ Click the **Paste Options** smart tag at the bottom of the chart.

Ⓑ Click **Keep Source Formatting & Link Data**.

15. Save the Word file.

16. Exit Excel, saving changes when prompted.

Open Excel and Chart Tools from Word

When data or objects from other sources are linked to Word documents, you can open source program tools directly from the Word document and use the tools to edit the object. Or, you can open the Excel application from within Word.

DEVELOP YOUR SKILLS: W12-D3

In this exercise, you will launch Excel from within Word and edit data in the worksheet. Then you will use Live Preview with Excel Chart Tools on the Word Ribbon to view potential formatting changes.

1. Save your file as **W12-D3-BudgetRpt**.

2. Double-click anywhere in the Excel worksheet table object to open the Excel file.

   At this stage, you can make editing changes that will be reflected in the Word document.

3. In Excel, click the Q1 cell for Staff Salaries (**cell B7**), type **1,000**, and tap Enter.

4. Switch to Word and ensure that the data and chart both updated.

   If your table failed to update, right-click the Excel worksheet table and choose Update Link from the menu. It's possible the worksheet table will update but not the chart. If your chart failed to update, double-click the chart and from the Ribbon choose Chart Tools→Design→Data→Refresh Data.

5. Switch to Excel and click **Undo** �.

6. Switch to Word.

   The chart and the worksheet data update to their original values. If your table failed to update, right-click the Excel worksheet table and choose Update Link from the menu. It's possible that the worksheet table will update but not the chart. If your chart failed to update, double-click the chart and choose Chart Tools→Design→Data→Refresh Data.

7. If you did not use Chart Tools in the previous step, double-click the chart to display the Chart Tools on the Ribbon.

8. Click the border of the chart to select the chart background.

   You should not see handles on objects within the border.

9. Choose **Chart Tools→Format→Shape Styles→Shape Fill 🖌 menu button ▾**.

10. Hover the mouse pointer over several different colors to see Live Preview display the effects as they impact the chart area background color.

11. Tap ⎡Esc⎤ to close the gallery and then tap ⎡Esc⎤ again to deselect the chart.

    The Chart Tools tabs disappear from the Ribbon.

12. Save and then close the Word file but leave the Excel file open.

Updating and Breaking Links

Linked objects in Word automatically update if the destination file is open at the time the source document changes. Naturally, the destination file is not always open when you modify the Excel source document; however, Word will prompt you to update links when you open a document containing links.

You can break the link between a linked object and its source document. Once the final figures for a period are in, you may want to break the link between Word and Excel so that the linked object is converted to an embedded object. Then, the Word report always reflects the closing numbers for that period.

DEVELOP YOUR SKILLS: W12-D4

In this exercise, you will modify the linked Excel file and observe the prompt to update links when you open the Word document. Then you will break the links to the worksheet data and test to see that the links are broken.

1. In Excel, click **cell C4** (Mortgage & Insurance for Q2), type **50,000**, and tap ⎡Enter⎤.

   You entered an overly large number so that the changes in the associated worksheet table and chart will be easy to see.

2. Open **W12-D3-BudgetRpt**, which contains the linked objects.

3. When the message appears prompting you to update links, click Yes.

   Observe the change in the worksheet data and in the chart. If your table failed to update, right-click the Excel worksheet table and choose Update Link from the menu. It's possible the worksheet table will update but not the chart. If your chart failed to update, click the chart border and choose Chart Tools→Design→Data→Refresh Data.

4. Save the Word file as **W12-D4-BudgetRpt**.

   Now you will break the link between the objects in Word and the Excel file.

5. In Word, right-click in the worksheet data to display a pop-up menu.

6. Slide the mouse pointer down to **Linked Worksheet Object** and choose **Links** from the submenu.

7. Follow these steps to break the link for the table:

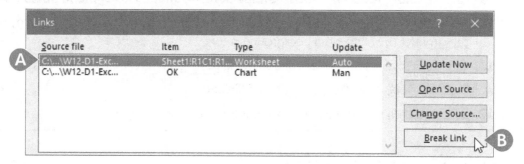

Ⓐ Make sure the worksheet object is selected.

Ⓑ Click **Break Link**.

8. When the message appears asking if you want to break the link, click **Yes**.

   The link disappears from the Links dialog box. The remaining link is already highlighted.

9. Click the **Break Link** button to break the link between Excel and the chart.

10. When the message box appears, click **Yes**.

    The Source File now displays the term NULL, indicating there is no source file attached.

11. Click **OK** to close the Links dialog box.

    Now you will test to see that the links are broken.

12. Right-click the worksheet object, review the menu options, and note that the Update Links option is gone.

13. Double-click the chart, choose **Chart Tools→Design→Data**, and notice that the Refresh Data button is grayed out, indicating that the link is broken.

14. Save and close the Word and Excel files but leave the program windows open.

Using Excel as a Mail Merge Data Source

You may recall the Word's Mail Merge feature is most often used for generating personalized form letters. Word can use a variety of file types as data sources, including Excel files. Whether you type a new data-source list from within Word or create your data source in Excel, the rules for effective data sources apply.

The more data is split into small segments, the more flexibility you have in the merge. A rule to remember is that you cannot merge part of a field. If the name field, for example, contains the title, first name, and last name, you will not be able to use those elements separately. For instance, in the greeting line, you will not be able to drop the first name and use Dear Title Last Name.

In Excel, the columns are treated as separate fields in a mail merge. Therefore, in a name and address list, it is a good idea to place the title, first name, and last name in separate columns, as shown in the following illustration.

	A	B	C	D	E	F	G
1	Title	First Name	Last Name	Address	City	State	Zip
2	Ms.	Sally	Redding	756 Locust Street	Los Angeles	CA	91025
3	Mr.	Jose	Lopez	7812 Olive Road	Los Angeles	CA	91357
4	Mr.	Charles	Douglas	91 Sycamore Ave.	Los Angeles	CA	91642

 When an Excel file is used as a merge data source file, the first row of the worksheet must contain the field names. In addition, all columns and rows must be adjacent to each other for Mail Merge to identify all entries as part of the same data source. You cannot have blank rows and columns within the Excel worksheet data.

≣ Mailings→Start Mail Merge→Select Recipients→Use an Existing List

DEVELOP YOUR SKILLS: W12-D5

In this exercise, you will begin by examining the Excel worksheet that you will use as the data source. Next you will open a letter and designate it as the main document. Then you will connect the Excel data source to the letter and conduct the merge.

1. In Excel, open **W12-D5-CommAddress** from your **Word Chapter 12** folder.

   Each column represents a mail merge field; Title is a field, First Name is a field, and so forth.

2. Look at the bottom of the Excel worksheet and notice the tab labeled Sheet 1.

   This is the name of the page in the Excel workbook that contains the address list. You will see Sheet 1 again later in this exercise.

3. Exit Excel.

4. In Word, open **W12-D5-CommLtr** and save it as **W12-D5-CommLtrRevised**.

5. Choose **Mailings→Start Mail Merge→Start Mail Merge** 🖺 and then choose **Letters**.

   This designates the letter as the main document.

6. If necessary, display formatting marks.

   Being able to see the formatting marks will be helpful later in this exercise. Now you will connect to the Excel data source.

7. Choose **Mailings→Start Mail Merge→Select Recipients** 🖾 and then choose **Use an Existing List**.

8. Navigate to your **Word Chapter 12** folder and open **W12-D5-CommAddress**.

9. When the Select Table dialog box appears, notice that Sheet 1 is highlighted.

   Earlier you observed Sheet 1 as the name of the page in the Excel workbook that contains the address list.

10. Click **OK**.

11. In the letter, select the **Today's Date** text; delete it but don't delete the paragraph symbol at the end of the line.

    Deleting the paragraph symbol would throw off proper business letter spacing.

12. Type the current date in its place.

Insert Merge Codes

13. Select and delete the **Address Block** text but don't delete the paragraph symbol at the end of the line.

14. Choose **Mailings→Write & Insert Fields→Address Block** 📄.

15. When the Insert Address Block dialog box appears, click **OK** to accept the default settings for the inside address.

16. Delete the **Greeting Line** text but not the paragraph symbol at the end of the line.

17. Choose **Mailings→Write & Insert Fields→Greeting Line** 📄.

18. When the Insert Greeting Line dialog box appears, change the Greeting Line Format from a comma to a colon and click **OK**.

Conduct the Merge

19. Choose **Mailings→Finish→Finish & Merge** 📄 and then choose **Edit Individual Documents**.

20. When the Merge to New Document dialog box opens, click **OK** to merge all of the records from the Excel file.

21. Turn off formatting marks and scroll through the letters to see the results of the merge.

22. Close the merge document without saving it.

23. Save and close **W12-D5-CommLtrRevised**.

Integrating Word with PowerPoint

PowerPoint is another program that Word can share files with. Word outlines can be used to create PowerPoint presentations. This hierarchical structure uses Heading 1 topics as the slide's title and headings such as Heading 2, Heading 3, and so forth as the bullet and sub-bullet entries in the slide.

Using Word Outline View

The following illustration is an example of an outline created specifically for generating a Power-Point presentation. Clicking or selecting entries in the outline displays the Word heading level in the Outlining tab on the Ribbon.

This field displays the Word heading style level of the highlighted heading.

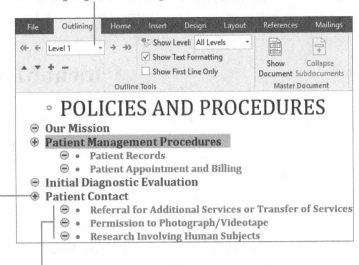

The plus (+) symbol indicates that there are lower-level headings below this heading.

Minus (-) symbols indicate that there are no lower-level headings below this heading.

Although you can use an existing document that contains Word headings to create a PowerPoint presentation, PowerPoint cannot extract just the headings from a document, so if you use an existing document with body text in addition to the headings, you will have to edit the PowerPoint presentation accordingly.

The procedures used to launch PowerPoint are the same as those used to launch Word. No special knowledge of PowerPoint is required to complete the following exercise.

≡ View→Views→Outline

DEVELOP YOUR SKILLS: W12-D6

In this exercise, you will use a Word outline to create a PowerPoint presentation. Then you will observe how the different heading levels are displayed in the presentation.

1. Open **W12-D6-ProcOutline** from your **Word Chapter 12** folder.
2. Choose **View→Views→Outline** 📄.
3. Click several different entries in the outline and notice the Word heading level indicated on the Ribbon.
4. Close the document and start PowerPoint.
5. Click the **Blank Presentation** template on the PowerPoint Start screen to open the PowerPoint window.
6. Choose **File→Open** and navigate to your **Word Chapter 12** folder.
7. In the bottom-right corner of the Open dialog box, click the file type drop-down list and choose **All Files (*.*)**.

8. Double-click **W12-D6-ProcOutline** to open it.

9. Follow these steps to display a slide containing a title and bullet points:

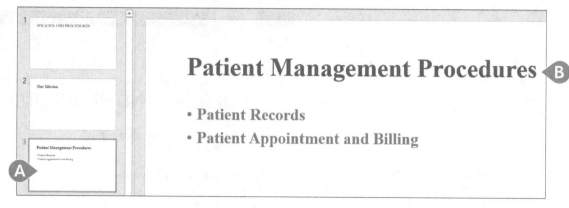

- (A) Click the third slide in the panel on the left.
- (B) This title was formatted using the Heading 1 style, and the bullet points are formatted using the Heading 2 style.

10. Exit PowerPoint without saving the file.

Adding a PowerPoint Presentation to a Word Document

When you create a document that will be distributed electronically, it could be useful to include a PowerPoint presentation within the document. For example, suppose you want to distribute a presentation and include a letter with it. You can create the letter and place the presentation in the body of the letter.

 When you insert a presentation into a Word document, only the first slide appears in the document. Double-clicking the slide image plays the show automatically.

≡ Insert→Text→Object→Create from File

DEVELOP YOUR SKILLS: W12-D7

In this exercise, you will insert a presentation into the letter being sent to board members.

1. Open **W12-D7-AdvisoryLtr** from your **Word Chapter 12** folder and save it as **W12-D7-AdvisoryLtrRevised**.

2. Turn on formatting marks and then position the insertion point in the middle paragraph symbol just before the complimentary close for the letter.

3. Choose **Insert→Text→Object** 🔲 and click the **Create from File** tab.

4. Click **Browse** and navigate to your **Word Chapter 12** folder.

5. Double-click **W12-D7-IntroToRCE.ppt** (a PowerPoint file) and then click **OK**.

Word adds a picture of the first slide in the letter. Notice that the image is large and makes the letter extend to two pages. Next you will size the image so that the letter fits on one page.

6. Click the slide image to display the sizing handles.

7. Drag the lower-right sizing handle diagonally up toward the center of the image until the letter fits on one page.

8. Double-click the slide image in the letter to start the slide show.

9. Click the mouse pointer anywhere on the screen to advance the slides.

10. When the black screen appears at the end of the show, click one more time to close it.

11. Save and close the file.

Opening, Editing, and Saving a PDF File

You can open, edit, and save a PDF file in Word 2016 without purchasing and learning separate, and often expensive, editing software. After editing the file, you can save it as a Word or PDF file. The file you open is considered a read-only file, so you must save it under a different name.

You can optimize a PDF file when you save it based on how your audience will likely read the file. And there are additional options, such as the range of pages you want to save and the ability to create bookmarks in the PDF file.

Choose additional publishing options here.

If your audience will be printing the PDF file, leave the option at Standard. If the file will be viewed only online, you can choose the Minimum Size option.

DEVELOP YOUR SKILLS: W12-D8

In this exercise, you will open a PDF file in Word and make editing changes. You will then resave the file as a PDF.

1. Choose **File→Open**, navigate to your **Word Chapter 12** folder, and open **W12-D8-PressRel**.

2. When the message appears, take a moment to read it and then click **OK**.

The PDF file opens with all the Word editing and formatting tools available.

Note! *When you open a PDF file in Word, there may be formatting issues. Don't worry about that now. Concentrate on opening so, in the future, you know how to open and edit a PDF file for which you don't have the original Word file.*

3. Select the three lines at the top of the page.

4. Choose **Home→Font→Font Color** [A] **menu button** ▾ and choose **Blue, Accent 1, Darker 25%**.

5. Choose **Home**→**Font**→**Font Size** and choose **16 pt**.

6. Choose **File**→**Save As**, navigate to your **Word Chapter 12** folder, save the file as **W12-D8-PressRelRevised**, choose **PDF (*.pdf)** from the Save as Type list, and then click **Save**.

7. If the PDF file opens in a PDF reader, close the PDF window.

   Remember, the original file is read-only, so saving it under a different name saved the changes in a new file.

8. The original file is still open in Word; close the file without saving.

Creating Web Pages from Word Documents

You can create web pages from Word documents. As you might imagine, this saves you the need to learn a more specialized web design or coding program. Another advantage is that Word can display a document in Web Layout view so you can make edits before posting the file on the web.

Format Web Pages

Web pages are often set up in tables to help align text in multiple columns, and the Table feature works well for this purpose. When you save a document as a web page, Word converts it to hypertext markup language (HTML), the authoring language for web pages. When you convert a document to HTML, some formatting features may be lost. However, most of your documents should translate cleanly into attractive web pages.

Add Alternative Text

Using alternative text helps people with limited vision understand the meaning of pictures and graphics. Although traditionally used with web pages, you can also add alternative text to regular Word documents for greater accessibility.

If a person uses a screen reader while viewing a web page, alternative text appears when hovering the mouse pointer over a picture or graphic. Some users won't see the text, but they'll hear it.

DEVELOP YOUR SKILLS: W12-D9

In this exercise, you will save a document as a web page and examine its format. You will also add alternative text to a picture in the document.

1. Open **W12-D9-RCEWalk** from your **Word Chapter 12** folder and save it as **W12-D9-RCEWalkRevised**.

2. If no gridlines appear, choose **Table Tools**→**Layout**→**Table**→**View Gridlines**.

   The document is set up in a table. The gridlines are visible so you can see the column with no content on the left side of the table. Web pages may appear too far to the left in a browser window, so the blank column is acting as a spacer to position the content farther to the right.

   Now you will add alternative text to the picture.

3. Right-click the picture and choose **Format Picture** to open the Format Picture task pane.

4. Follow these steps to add alternative text:

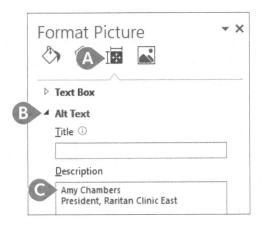

Ⓐ Click the **Layout & Properties** button.

Ⓑ Click **Alt Text**.

Ⓒ Type this text in the description field.

Note! *The title field should be filled in only if you are entering a detailed explanation in the Description field.*

5. Close the Format Picture task pane.

6. Choose **File→Save As** and navigate to your **Word Chapter 12** folder.

7. Follow these steps to set the format and title of the web page document:

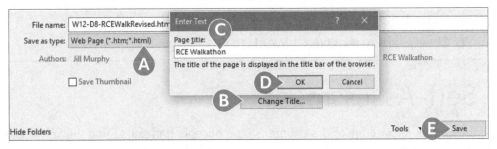

Ⓐ Choose **Web Page (*.htm;*html)** from the Save as Type drop-down list.

Ⓑ Click the **Change Title** button to open the Enter Text dialog box.

Ⓒ Type **RCE Walkathon** in the Page Title field.

Ⓓ Click **OK**.

Ⓔ Click **Save**.

8. Launch Internet Explorer or your default browser.

   Steps for opening the file in your default browser may vary slightly. You may need to seek assistance to determine the correct method.

9. Press Ctrl+O and click the **Browse** button.

10. Navigate to your **Word Chapter 12** folder, double-click **W12-D9-RCEWalkRevised.htm**, and click **OK**.

    If you do not see the .htm file extension, look closely, and you will see that the web page file has a slightly different icon than a Word file icon.

11. Review the document layout and notice that the gridlines do not appear.

12. Close the browser and the Word web page file.

Edit Web Pages in Word

When you create a web page in Word, you can use Word to edit the page as well. You open the *.htm* page from within Word, make the necessary changes, and then resave the file. When you open it in the browser again, you will see the editing changes that you made.

DEVELOP YOUR SKILLS: W12-D10

In this exercise, you will open the web page you created in the previous exercise and edit it. Then you will reopen the page in your browser and observe the change.

1. Open **W12-D9-RCEWalkRevised.htm**.

   If you do not see the .htm file extension, look closely, and you will see that the web page file has a slightly different icon than a Word file icon.

2. Change the walkathon date from March 1 to March **8**.

3. Save and close the file and then restart your browser.

   Steps for opening the file in your default browser may vary slightly. You may need to seek assistance to determine the correct method.

4. Press ⌈Ctrl⌉+⌈O⌉ and navigate to your **Word Chapter 12** folder.

5. Double-click **W12-D9-RCEWalkRevised.htm** and click **OK**.

6. Observe the date change you made in the web page.

7. Close your browser and exit Word.

Self-Assessment

 Check your knowledge of this chapter's key concepts and skills using the Self-Assessment in your ebook or eLab course.

Reinforce Your Skills

REINFORCE YOUR SKILLS: W12-R1

Create a Consignment Shop Sales Report

Kids for Change operates a fund-raising consignment shop, Collectibles & Curiosities. In this exercise, you will prepare a static sales report and distribute it to the board members and then link the sales report data so you can start collecting data for your year-to-date report.

1. Start Word, open **W12-R1-Q1SalesRpt** from your **Word Chapter 12** folder, and save it as **W12-R1-Q1SalesRptRevised**.

2. Position the insertion point in the first blank line below the paragraph.

3. If necessary, choose **View→Views→Print Layout** 📄 to change from Web Layout view.

4. If necessary, turn on formatting marks, choose **Insert→Text→Object** 🔲, and click the **Create from File** tab.

5. Click **Browse**, navigate to your **Word Chapter 12** folder, and double-click **W12-R1-Collectibles**.

   Because you are embedding (not linking) the data in Word, you won't check the Link to File checkbox.

6. Click **OK** to close the dialog box and insert the table.

   Having distributed this report to the board members, you will now link this worksheet table in the Word document so you can begin collecting year-to-date data.

7. Click the embedded worksheet table and tap [Delete].

Link Excel Data to a Word Document

8. Start Excel, click the **Open Other Workbooks** link at the bottom of the Recent list on the left of the Start screen, and navigate to your **Word Chapter 12** folder.

9. Open **W12-R1-Collectibles** and save it as **W12-R1-CollectiblesRevised**.

10. Make sure the **Collectibles and Curiosities** merged cell is selected and then press [Shift] and click the last cell in the table (value of **$1,464.00**).

11. Choose **Home→Clipboard→Copy**, switch to Word, and position the insertion point in the first blank line below the main paragraph.

12. Choose **Home→Clipboard→Paste menu button** ▼ **→Paste Special**.

13. In the Paste Special dialog box, choose **Microsoft Excel Worksheet Object**, click the **Paste Link** option, and click **OK**.

    Now you will edit the worksheet in Excel and observe the change in the linked table.

14. Switch to Excel, tap [Esc] to remove the marquee surrounding the table, and click the cell at the top of the worksheet to select it.

15. Double-click the cell to position the insertion point in the cell and then click and drag to select **Quarter 1**.

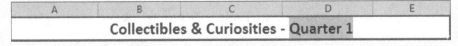

16. Type **Year-to-Date**, tap Enter, and then switch to **Word**.

    Notice that the linked table updated with the change you made. If the table failed to update, right-click it and choose Update Link.

17. Position the insertion point on the blank line below the table.

    Now you will link an Excel chart in Word using the Paste Options smart tag.

18. Switch to Excel, click the **Sheet 2** tab at the bottom of the workbook, and then click the chart to select it.

19. Choose **Home→Clipboard→Copy** and then switch back to Word.

20. Choose **Home→Clipboard→Paste** and click the **Paste Options** smart tag at the bottom of the chart.

21. Click the **Keep Source Formatting & Link Data** button. (If necessary, use ToolTips to identify the button.)

22. Switch to Excel, exit Excel, and save changes when prompted.

Open Excel and Display Chart Tools from Within Word

23. Double-click in the worksheet table in Word to open the Excel file.

    You realize that there is an error in the March sales figure for Glass & Crystal, so you will make that change in the worksheet.

24. Click **cell B7** (Glass & Crystal, March), tap Delete, type **1,500.00**, and tap Enter.

25. Switch to Word and ensure that the table and chart both updated.

    If your table failed to update, right-click the Excel worksheet table and choose Update Link from the menu. It's possible the worksheet table will update but not the chart. If your chart failed to update, click the chart and choose Chart Tools→Design→Data→Refresh Data.

26. Save the document and exit Word.

Update Links and Break a Link Between Word and Excel

27. In Excel, click to select **cell D5** (Vintage Jewelry, January), tap Delete, type **600**, and tap Enter.

28. In Word, open **W12-R1-Q1SalesRptRevised**; when the message appears prompting you to update links, click **Yes**.

29. If your table or chart failed to update, use the manual procedures you've used before to update.

30. In Word, right-click the worksheet table to display the pop-up menu.

31. Slide the mouse pointer down to **Linked Worksheet Object** and choose **Links** from the submenu.

32. With the worksheet selected, click **Break Link**.

33. When the message appears verifying the break, click **Yes**.

34. With the chart selected, click **Break Link**, click **Yes**, and then click **OK**.

    Now you will test to ensure that the links are broken.

35. Right-click the **worksheet table** in Word and notice that Update Links does not appear in the menu.

36. Select the chart and choose **Chart Tools→Design→Data** and notice that the Refresh Data button is grayed out.

37. Save and close the Word and Excel files.

Organize an Autumn Garden Cleanup for Seniors

Kids for Change volunteers assist senior citizens with autumn garden cleanup every year, and it's time to get that project rolling again. In this exercise, you will use Excel and Mail Merge to send letters announcing the volunteers' meeting. You will also convert a Word outline to a PowerPoint presentation for the meeting to review garden tasks needed at this time of the year. And finally, you will save a document as a web page so volunteers can go online to see which gardening supplies are needed for the project.

1. Open **W12-R2-GardenLtr** from your **Word Chapter 12** folder and save it as **W12-R2-GardenLtrRevised**.

2. Choose **Mailings→Start Mail Merge→Start Mail Merge** 📄**→Letters**.

   Word will now recognize your letter as the main document.

3. If necessary, turn on formatting marks.

   Now you will connect an Excel file as the data source.

4. Choose **Mailings→Start Mail Merge→Select Recipients** and then choose **Use an Existing List**.

5. Navigate to your **Word Chapter 12** folder and open **W12-R2-AddressLst.xls** (an Excel file).

6. When the Select Table dialog box appears, make sure **Sheet 1**, which contains the address list, is selected and then click **OK**.

   Now you will insert the merge codes in your letter.

7. In the letter, delete the **Address Block** text but not the paragraph symbol at the end of the line.

8. Choose **Mailings→Write & Insert Fields→Address Block** 📄.

9. When the Insert Address Block dialog box opens, click **OK** to accept the default formats for the inside address.

10. Delete the **Greeting Line** text but not the paragraph symbol at the end of the line.

11. Choose **Mailings→Write & Insert Fields→Greeting Line** 📄.

12. When the Insert Greeting Line dialog box opens, choose **Joshua** from the drop-down list and click **OK** to insert the Greeting Line code.

    Now you will conduct the merge.

13. Choose **Mailings→Finish→Finish & Merge** 📄**→Edit Individual Documents**.

14. When the Merge to New Document dialog box opens, click **OK** and then turn off formatting marks.

15. Scroll through the documents to see the results of the merge and then close the document without saving it.

16. Save and close **W12-R2-GardenLtrRevised**.

Create a PowerPoint Presentation from a Word Outline

Now you will create the PowerPoint presentation that Kids for Change will use during the meeting to remind team members of the various gardening tasks that must be completed during their cleanup project. You will generate the presentation from a Word outline.

17. Open **W12-R2-GardenTasks** and choose **View→Views→Outline**.

18. Click several different entries and notice the heading levels indicated on the Ribbon.

Level 1 entries will provide slide titles, and Level 2 entries will provide bullet points.

19. Close the outline document.

20. Start PowerPoint and click the **Open Other Presentations** link at the bottom of the Recent list on the left of the Start screen.

21. Navigate to your **Word Chapter 12** folder; in the bottom-right corner, click the drop-down list and choose **All Files (*.*)**.

22. Double-click **W12-R2-GardenTasks**.

23. Click several slide icons in the left panel and notice that the titles are formed from the Level 1 outline entries and the bullet points come from the Level 2 outline entries.

24. Exit PowerPoint without saving.

Save a Document as a Web Page

In planning for the Kids for Change garden cleanup project, the project manager needs to determine which gardening supplies members can contribute to use during the project.

25. Open **W12-R2-GardenSupplies** from your **Word Chapter 12** folder and save it as `W12-R2-GardenSuppliesRevised`.

The document is set up in a table, which is common for organizing data in web pages. If you cannot see table gridlines, choose Table Tools→Layout→Table→View Gridlines.

26. Choose **File→Save As**, navigate to your **Word Chapter 12** folder, and choose **Web Page (*.htm,*.html)** from the Save as Type list.

27. Click the **Change Title** button, type `Gardening Supplies` in the dialog box, and click **OK**.

This text will appear in the title bar or as a tab in your default browser.

28. Click **Save**, and Word automatically switches to Web Layout view.

Now you will open the document in your web browser. Steps for opening the file in your default browser may vary slightly. You may need to seek assistance to determine the correct method.

29. Start your browser, press Ctrl+O, and click **Browse**.

30. Navigate to your **Word Chapter 12** folder and double-click **W12-R2-GardenSuppliesRevised**. (If necessary, use the file icon to identify the web page file.)

31. Observe the *Gardening Supplies* at the top of the browser and then close the browser.

32. Exit all programs.

Report on a Fund-Raiser and Work on Pending Projects

Kids for Change sells used books to raise funds for its projects. In this exercise, you will send a letter to the board members containing sales data from Excel. And you will use a PDF file, a PowerPoint presentation, and a web page to help pending projects move forward.

1. Start Word, open **W12-R3-BookSalesLtr** from your **Word Chapter 12** folder, and save it as **W12-R3-BookSalesLtrRevised**.

2. If necessary, choose **View→Views→Print Layout** to change from Web Layout view.

3. Start Excel and click the **Open Other Workbooks** link at the bottom of the Recent list on the left side of the Start screen.

4. Navigate to your **Word Chapter 12** folder, open **W12-R3-UsedBookSales**, and save it as **W12-R3-UsedBookSalesRevised**.

5. Press Ctrl + Home to select the first cell in the worksheet and press Shift and click the last cell in the table (**$1,424.00**).

6. Press Ctrl + C to copy the data.

7. Switch to Word, display formatting marks, and then position the insertion point on the second blank line below the letter closing.

8. Choose **Home→Clipboard→Paste menu button ▾→Paste Special**.

9. Choose **Microsoft Excel Worksheet Object** from the list, click the **Paste Link** option button, and click **OK**.

10. Close Excel.

    Now you will open Excel from within Word.

11. Double-click the worksheet table in Word to open the Excel file.

    You need to correct the January sales figure for Historical Fiction.

12. Click **cell C3** (Historical Fiction, January), type **$385.00**, and tap Enter.

13. Switch to Word and verify that the worksheet table updated.

14. If your table failed to update, right-click the table and choose **Update Link**.

15. Save and close the Word document and exit Excel, saving the file when prompted.

Add a PowerPoint Presentation to a Word Document

Kids for Change will soon meet to discuss upcoming projects. You will paste a PowerPoint presentation that overviews the projects into a letter to the board members for their review.

16. Open **W12-R3-BoardMtgLtr** from your **Word Chapter 12** folder and save it as **W12-R3-BoardMtgLtrRevised**.

17. Position the insertion point at the end of the document.

18. Choose **Insert→Text→Object** and click the **Create from File** tab.

19. Click **Browse**, navigate to your **Word Chapter 12** folder, double-click **W12-R3-ProjectsPPT.ppt**, and then click **OK**.

20. Double-click the slide image to start the presentation and then click the mouse pointer on the screen to advance the slides. (Notice the Beach Cleanup and Golden Retriever Rescue projects as you view the presentation.)

21. When the black screen appears, click again to close the presentation and then save and close the file.

Edit a PDF File in Word

One of the upcoming projects is Beach Cleanup. Kids for Change wants to get local school kids involved. You will send an online letter to superintendents in the area requesting their support in this mission. You will use a PDF file as it's likely that the letter will be read on computers with varying operating systems and software. The date for the cleanup has slipped a week, so you need to update the file.

22. In Word, open **W12-R3-SuperLtr.pdf** from your **Word Chapter 12** folder.

23. When the message appears, click **OK** and change the date (second line of body paragraph) from September 3rd to September **10th.**

24. Save the file as a PDF file naming it **W12-R3-SuperLtrRevised**.

25. If the file opens in a PDF reader, close the reader.

26. Close the Word document without saving.

Create a Web Page from a Word Document

One of the pending projects is the Golden Retriever Rescue project. You've created a flyer announcing the Foster Home Fair for Golden Retriever Rescue, which will take place at the Community Center. You will save it as a web page so it can be posted on the Community Center website.

27. Open **W12-R3-FosterHomeFair** from your **Word Chapter 12** folder.

28. Choose **File→Save As** and navigate to your **Word Chapter 12** folder.

29. Name the file **W12-R3-FosterHomeFairRevised** and choose **Web Page (*.htm,*html)** from the Save as Type list.

30. Click the **Change Title** button, type **Foster Home Fair**, click **OK**, and then click **Save**.

    Now you will add alternative text to the picture to enhance accessibility.

31. Right-click the picture and choose **Format Picture**.

32. In the Format Picture task pane, click the **Layout & Properties** button and then click **Alt Text**.

33. Type **Olivia needs a good home!** in the Description field and then close the **task pane**.

    Seek assistance if you need help opening the file in your browser.

34. Start your default web **browser**, press Ctrl+O, navigate to your **Word Chapter 12** folder, and double-click **W12-R3-FosterHomeFairRevised**.

35. Review the web page and then close the browser.

    Now you will edit the web page. The Word web page should still be open.

36. Position the insertion point at the end of the last bullet point, tap Enter, and type **Fire Department BBQ Cook-off**.

37. Save and close the file.

    Seek assistance if you need help opening the file in your browser.

38. Start your browser, press Ctrl+O, navigate to your **Word Chapter 12** folder, double-click **W12-R3-FosterHomeFairRevised**, and click **OK**.

39. Observe the change you made to the web page and then close the browser.

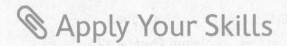 Apply Your Skills

APPLY YOUR SKILLS: W12-A1

Prepare a Report Comparing Tours

In this exercise, you will produce a report for the Universal Corporate Events management team comparing the sales of four tours over three months. You will embed an Excel worksheet table in a Word document and then link an Excel worksheet table and chart in the document. You will update links when changes are made in Excel, and finally you will break the link between Word and Excel.

1. Open **W12-A1-MgmtLtr** from your **Word Chapter 12** folder and save it as **W12-A1-MgmtLtrRevised**.

2. If necessary, choose **View→View→Print Layout** to change from Web Layout view.

3. If necessary, display formatting marks; then position the insertion point on the second blank line below the letter closing.

4. Start Excel, open **W12-A1-1stQSales** from your **Word Chapter 12** folder, and save it as **W12-A1-1stQSalesRevised.**

5. Press ⌈Ctrl⌉+⌈Home⌉ to select the cell at the top of the table, press ⌈Shift⌉, and click the last cell in the table, which displays the value of **$150,000**.

6. Copy the table and then switch to Word and make sure the insertion point is on the second blank line below the letter.

7. Click **Paste menu button ▾→Paste Special** and link the **Microsoft Excel Worksheet** object in Word.

   Now you will make a change to the Excel table and observe the change in the linked table in Word.

8. Switch to Excel and turn off the marquee.

9. Click **cell C3** (Hawaii Resort, January) and enter **40,000** to replace the current number.

10. Switch to Word and notice the change you made.

    If your worksheet table failed to update, use the Update Link command. Now you will link an Excel chart from the same file in the document.

11. In Excel, click the **Sheet 2** tab and then click the chart.

12. Copy the chart, switch to **Word** and paste it at the bottom of the document, and then use the **Paste Options smart tag** and the **Keep Source Formatting & Link Data** button to link the chart in Word.

13. Switch to Excel and save your changes; exit Excel.

    Now you will open Excel from within Word and edit the worksheet.

14. Double-click the worksheet table to open Excel and change the data in **cell B5** (Bahamas Cruise, March) to **45,000**.

15. Switch to Word, observe the change, and, if necessary, use **Update Link** to update the worksheet table and **Refresh Data** to update the chart.

16. Save and close the file; exit Word.

    Now you'll make a change in Excel and update links when you reopen the Word document.

17. In Excel, replace the data in **cell D4** (Florida Spa, February) with **40,000**.

18. Start Word, open **W12-A1-MgmtLtrRevised** from your **Word Chapter 12** folder, and update the links.

19. If necessary, use Update Link to update the worksheet table and Refresh Data to update the chart.

    Because you don't want the data to update any more, you will break the link between Word and Excel.

20. In the Links dialog box, break the link for both the worksheet and the chart.

21. Right-click the worksheet table and ensure that the Update Links command is not available.

22. Click the chart and choose **Chart Tools→Design→Data** and observe that the **Refresh Data** button is grayed out.

23. Save and close all files and exit Excel.

APPLY YOUR SKILLS: W12-A2

Prepare Documents for a Tour to Turkey

Universal Corporate Events reps are planning a tour of Turkey for a client. In this exercise, you will create a PowerPoint presentation from a Word outline. Then you will insert a PowerPoint presentation in a letter for tour members and create a web page from a Word document listing side tours in Turkey.

1. Open **W12-A2-TurkeyOutline** and switch to **Outline view**.

2. Observe the different heading levels indicated in the Outlining tab, which will become the title and bullet-point entries in the PowerPoint slides; close the outline document.

3. Start PowerPoint, click **Open Other Presentations** at the bottom of the left panel, and navigate to your **Word Chapter 12** folder.

4. In the bottom of the Open dialog box, choose **All Files (*.*)** from the drop-down list.

5. Double-click **W12-A2-TurkeyOutline** to open it; click through the slides in the left panel and observe the effect of the different heading levels in the outline.

6. Exit PowerPoint without saving.

    Now you will add a PowerPoint presentation to a letter you're sending as an email attachment to the tour members.

7. In Word, open **W12-A2-TurkeyLtr** from your **Word Chapter 12** folder and save it as **W12-A2-TurkeyLtrRevised**.

8. Position the insertion point at the end of the document, insert **W12-A2-TurkeyPPT.ppt**, and view the presentation.

    Now you will save the letter as a PDF file as tour members will likely have different types of computers.

9. Choose **File→Save As**, navigate to your **Word Chapter 12** folder, and save the file as a **PDF** file.

10. If your file opens in a PDF reader, close the reader.

11. Save and close **W12-A2-TurkeyLtrRevised.pdf**.

    The location for the meeting has changed, so you will edit the PDF file in Word and resave it as a PDF file.

12. Open the **PDF** file in Word and change *Lakeside* to **Harbor**.

13. Resave the file as a **PDF** file and name it **W12-A2-TurkeyLtrRevised2**.

14. If the file opens in a reader, close the reader.

15. Save the Word document as **W12-A2-TurkeyLtrRevised2**; make sure it's a *.docx* file and then close it.

Create and Edit a Web Page in Word

You have been asked to create a web page for the Universal Corporate Events website showing the side tours offered for the tour of Turkey.

16. Open **W12-A2-TurkeyWebPage**, save it as a **Web Page (*.htm,*.html)**, name it **W12-A2-TurkeyWebPageRevised**, and change the title to **Side Trips in Turkey**.

17. Open and observe the web page in your browser and then close the browser.

    Now you will add a side-tour destination to the web page. The web page document should still be open in Word.

18. Position the insertion point after *Turkish Bath*, tap Enter, and type **Istanbul**.

19. Save and close the file.

20. Open the file in your browser again, observe the change, and then close the browser.

APPLY YOUR SKILLS: W12-A3

Plan an Australian Tour

A Universal Corporate Events representative is preparing an Australian tour for a client. You have been asked to prepare the documents associated with the tour. In this exercise, you will use an Excel name and address list for a mail merge and prepare a letter containing a PowerPoint presentation. Then you will prepare a web page about Australia for tour members to view online.

1. Open **W12-A3-AustraliaLtr** from your **Word Chapter 12** folder and save it as **W12-A3-AustraliaLtrRevised**.

2. Designate the letter as the main document in a mail merge.

3. Designate **Sheet 1** of the **W12-A3-AustraliaN&A.xls** Excel file as the recipient list.

4. Replace the **Address Block** placeholder text with the **Address Block code**, accepting the default formats for the inside address.

5. Replace the **Greeting Line** placeholder text with the **Greeting Line code**, accepting the default formats for the greeting line.

6. Finish the merge, choosing **Edit Individual Documents**, and merge all records.

7. Review the merged letters and then close the merged file without saving.

8. Save and close **W12-A3-AustraliaLtrRevised**.

Insert a PowerPoint Presentation in a Word Document

The tour members have now attended an orientation meeting, and the Universal Corporate Events representative has asked you to insert the PowerPoint presentation in a letter to members so they can review the topics covered in the meeting.

9. Open **W12-A3-OrientLtr** from your **Word Chapter 12** folder and save it as **W12-A3-OrientLtrRevised**.

10. Position the insertion point at the end of the letter, insert **W12-A3-AussiePPT.ppt**, and view the presentation.

11. Save and close the file.

Create and Edit a Web Page in Word

12. Open **W12-A3-AussieWebPage** from your **Word Chapter 12** folder, save it as a web page, name it **W12-A3-AussieWebPageRevised**, and change the title to **Australia Overview**.

13. View the web page in your browser and then close the browser.

    Now you will edit the web page in Word. The web page file should still be open.

14. Position the insertion point after the word *Territories*, tap ⌷Enter⌷, type **History**, and then save and close the web page file.

15. View the web page in your browser, observe the change you made, and then close the browser.

16. Exit Word.

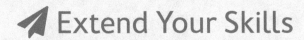 # Extend Your Skills

These exercises challenge you to think critically and apply your new skills. You will be evaluated on your ability to follow directions, completeness, creativity, and the use of proper grammar and mechanics. Save files to your chapter folder. Submit assignments as directed.

W12-E1 That's the Way I See It

As a sales rep for a small business, you track your quarterly sales in Excel. It's the end of the third quarter, and you will submit the end-of-quarter figures and the associated chart to your boss in a Word file. Create a one-paragraph Word file indicating that you are submitting your third-quarter sales summary. Name the file **W12-E1-MyLetter**. Link the worksheet table and chart from **W12-E1-3rdQSales**. The product names are generic. Decide which products your company sells and change the product names in the Excel file accordingly; update the linked objects in your Word document, too.

Your boss has asked you to use Mail Merge to send a mailing to customers announcing a new product. Decide on the new product and then write a letter (one to two paragraphs) describing it. Save the file as **W12-E1-MyMergeLtr**. Designate the letter as the main document and **W12-E1-Address** (Word Chapter 12 folder) as the recipient list. Add the Address Block and Greeting Line merge codes; conduct the merge. Save the merged file as **W12-E1-Merged**.

W12-E2 Be Your Own Boss

As the owner of Blue Jean Landscaping, you plan to hold a seminar to discuss your products and services. You want a PowerPoint presentation to guide your seminar. Use the Word outline **W12-E2-BJLGardens** to create the slides and save the presentation as **W12-E2-BJL-PPT**. After the seminar, you will email a Word document to attendees with the presentation inserted. Create a letter (1–2 paragraphs) thanking customers for attending the seminar. Note that the presentation is included, and add instructions on how to play the slide show. Save the Word document as **W12-E2-BJLLetter**. Save the document as a web page and test it in your browser.

W12-E3 Demonstrate Proficiency

Stormy BBQ sponsors an annual rodeo. To encourage a big turnout, you've been asked to prepare a PowerPoint presentation to use as an email attachment for Stormy's customers. To begin, open **W12-E3-RodeoOutline** in PowerPoint. Save the presentation as **W12-E3-RodeoPres**. Then create a two- or three-paragraph Word document describing the rodeo and why people should attend. Save the file as **W12-E3-RodeoWordDoc**. Insert a PowerPoint presentation, **W12-E3-RodeoPPT.ppt**, in the document. Remember to include instructions on how to run the slide show.

There will be a Rodeo Raffle, and you've been asked to create a web page to put on Stormy's website listing the prizes. Convert **W12-E3-RodeoWebPage** to a web page named **W12-E3-RodeoWebPage**. Test it in your browser. Add a prize, a $50 Starbuck's gift card, to the bottom of the list of prizes in the web document and then test it again in your browser.

Glossary

Accessibility Checker Tells you about possible accessibility issues in your files so you can fix them so someone with a disability can read and access your content

collaborating Working together with other people to edit and complete a document

Compatibility Checker When a Word 2016 document is saved down to Word 2010 or an even earlier version, the Compatibility Checker notifies the user how features specific to Word 2016 will be handled

Compatibility Mode Opening a document that was created in Word 2010 or earlier opens it in Compatibility Mode; available features are limited to those found in the earlier versions

Compatibility Pack This free download from Microsoft allows a user to open a Word 2016 or 2013 document in an earlier version of Word

convert Feature that allows you to transform documents that were created in an earlier version of an application to the Office 2016 file format

destination file A file on which an operation is performed or into which data copied from another document is pasted

digital signature Means of authenticating the identity of the originator of a document; a signed document cannot be modified

Document Inspector Reviews documents for hidden data or personal information

document properties Information about a document, such as the date and time it was last modified, the author's name, and the name of the last person who modified it

embed To incorporate within the body of a file or document

encryption Technique for encoding a document so it can only be read by the sender and the intended recipient

link A code or instruction that connects one part of a source file to a destination file; the destination file can be updated when the source file is modified

Macro A series of frequently used commands grouped together and saved as a single command; used to speed up repetitive tasks

Mark as Final Command that makes a document read-only; places an icon on the status bar to let readers know they are viewing the final form of the document

object Refers to graphical images such as shapes, WordArt, Excel spreadsheets, charts, and pictures; these elements can be shared between documents

One Drive A service offered by Microsoft that provides free online storage to those who have a Microsoft Account ID; allows you to get and share files from anywhere on any device

round-tripping Converting a document created in Word 97-2003 to Word 2016 format and then saving it back to the Word 97-2003 document format

source file The document in which data or copied text originally appeared

Visual Basic for Applications (VBA) A programming language used by Office programs that creates modules containing macros

Index

Note: Page numbers ending with a "V" indicate that a term is discussed in the video referenced on that page.